IN THE SHADOW OF
GIANTS

IN THE SHADOW OF
GIANTS

A HEARTFELT JOURNEY INTO THE
MOST FAMOUS SMALL FAN BASES
OF EUROPEAN FOOTBALL

LEANDRO VIGNOLI

First published by Pitch Publishing, 2021

Pitch Publishing
A2 Yeoman Gate
Yeoman Way
Worthing
Sussex
BN13 3QZ
www.pitchpublishing.co.uk
info@pitchpublishing.co.uk

A CIP catalogue record is available for this book
from the British Library.

ISBN 978-1-78531-887-0

Typesetting and origination by Pitch Publishing
Printed and bound in India by Replika Press Pvt. Ltd.

CONTENTS

You can change your wife, your politics, your religion, but never can you change your football team.
— **Eric Cantona**

Why couldn't you beat a richer club? I've never seen a bag of money score a goal.
— **Johan Cruyff**

It's not about how hard you hit. It's about how hard you can get hit and keep moving forward.
— **Rocky Balboa**

PREFACE

What is it like to support a team that never wins?

I asked this question to football fans all around Europe during a 50-day trip attending games. However, what I quickly discovered is that there is no single answer. And perhaps, more importantly, there is no perfect answer. When we fall in love with a team, normally when we're young, it's for a combination of reasons. These reasons may disappear as we get older: supporting a football team is a lifelong commitment that most people are not keen on. However, sometimes those reasons grow even bigger, and they develop into fervent passion. That's when we're ready to have our hearts broken.

The act of supporting a team is not rational, just like when you fall in love with someone. People tend to look for their soulmates through common tastes, in music, movies, books, or even a compatible lifestyle, like if the other person is a night owl or not. And all of a sudden one finds the perfect person, who happens to like fuckin' James Blunt and Jennifer Aniston movies, while one would rather listen to Slayer all day and watch all the Mad Max sequels. Just like sometimes the football team that you love happens to be absolute *shite*. True love is like that.

I know how this analogy sounds long-winded to some of you, but diehard football fans *will refer* to their support as love, which is not something objective that can be explained. Neuroscientists have tried to, and poets have dedicated their lives to it, so I'm guessing you will not find the answers to love in a football book. Nonetheless, here I am and nobody can stop me from trying.

There is a substantial difference, though, when it comes to loving a football team. It doesn't require retribution. All the things that we do – attending matches, collecting jerseys, suffering when they lose – revolve around the idea that our team will always be there for us no matter what. Especially during their big losses, that is, when we've earned the badge of a true fan. When one is committed to teams that constantly fail, there is a bigger sense of pride, of not jumping on the team bandwagon only when they're winning.

However, this is the trickier part in terms of fan culture. There *are* fans that beg for retribution. One can even argue that the majority of football fans want retribution. Winning titles is a major factor for so many fans to pick a team to support, especially, but not exclusively, at a young age. Even when we start supporting a traditional club being seen as a sleeping giant. Eventually many of us will ask for something back and there is no shame in admitting it. Regardless of the particular situation, it is the optimism to win one day that keeps us going.

I have chosen small teams from Europe because the leagues' winners are extremely scarce when compared with others. In Brazil, six different teams have won the league since 2010, for example. Eight different teams have won the Argentine league, and nine different teams have won the Copa Libertadores in the last ten years. Meanwhile in Spain, Real Madrid and Barcelona have won nine of the last ten titles; PSG have won seven of the last eight in France; Bayern Munich won eight straight in Germany; Juventus nine in a row in Italy. Even the English 'Big Six' has been reduced to three champions in the last decade. It is unlikely that any of these teams will ever spend more than a couple of seasons without celebrating a trophy. Their fan base is plentiful.

This is the part of the story where I remember supporters that I spoke with at every stadium. They chanted, and cried, and took me to drink beer so they could endlessly talk about their teams, their fan bases, their region and friends. They could not talk about any titles. It is a very different experience from supporting a big club, where defeats are regarded as humiliations. These fan bases see football through the pain that accompanies the losses. There are millions of people supporting a small team, even if we barely notice them. When someone supports Rayo Vallecano in Madrid, to name just one club that I visited, their choice is not only born out of passion, but an act of resistance. It's like surviving in a place where they have been left to die. These fan bases are holding an umbrella during a hurricane.

Not only do they support a small team, but the economic gap in modern football has significantly increased in the last years. The difference in budgets has made people adopt slogans such as 'Against Modern Football', or to believe that it is 'more than just football'. However, many of these fan bases covered in this book are not against the modernisation of football per se. It is not only nostalgia. This is literally the only alternative left.

All the clubs in this book come from cities where they have a much bigger neighbour; they are in the shadow of giants. Clubs like Espanyol, also known as 'the other team from Barcelona'; Rayo Vallecano, Madrid's working-class football club; Belenenses, from the historic village of Belém in Lisbon. I have visited three different clubs in London: Millwall, due to their reputation for hooliganism; Fulham, due to their reputation as being a 'friendly club'; and Leyton Orient, due to their reputation for ... well, they have no reputation.

Then I visited Red Star, a traditional and decadent team from Paris; Sparta, a traditional and decadent team from Rotterdam; and 1860 Munich, a traditional and decadent team in Munich. I finished this trip in Turin, where Torino is definitely a club full of glories and tradition, but in a constant fight with their tragic past, and present days of voilà decadence.

I added three more clubs almost literally while packing, either because I heard a fascinating story or – let's be honest – they were geographically too close to resist attending a match. I visited Queen's Park from Glasgow, the oldest club in the country; Union Berlin, a former East German team with a legacy of resistance to the socialist regime and the Stasi; and in Hamburg, I went to St. Pauli, a notorious Antifa-supported club.

I spent 1,440 minutes inside football stadiums, watched 15 games and 35 goals scored, with a total attendance of 275,000 fans. This is the equivalent of spending 24 hours straight watching football on TV (and I'm not talking about UEFA Champions League level). I travelled 11,000 kilometres (6,835 miles) on buses, trains, planes and cars, a longer distance than my original flight from São Paulo to Madrid. During the coldest evenings, watching some matches reminded me of how I used to feel when I needed to work extra hours after a long carnival weekend of drinking and partying, that feeling of 'I really want to go home'.

And why did I do it exactly? Well, because I am a football fanatic capable of watching Tahiti vs New Caledonia at 4am for no reason. Moreover, however, I am a *diehard fan of a football team*. Don't get me wrong, but enjoying the beautiful game and supporting a team is not the same thing. There is a subtle but fundamental difference when we feel like we are part of the game, like the indescribable anxiety before a penalty shoot-out only when our team is involved.

I don't support a small team myself, in case you're wondering. I grew up in the Porto Alegre area as an Internacional fan following in the steps of my father, who passed away when I was little. Recently, Inter won the Copa Libertadores twice, and they won three leagues in the 1970s. When I began attending games aged 12, however, this success was remote. The team was rubbish for more than a decade and I felt trapped, with my entire youth supporting a team with useless hope, and to make matters worse, our biggest rivals in the city, Grêmio (argh!), had won everything that was possible. Eventually all that misery and suffering was reversed, as we started winning titles and Grêmio were relegated to the second division twice (too bad, too bad), but all those years I spent attending rainy evening games that we lost to lower-division teams in the Brazilian Cup is what really moulded me into the supporter I am today.

The entire concept of this book came about as a curiosity to understand the resilience required to support a team that never wins. Where your fearless rivals are Goliath, and you can't even brag about being David. However, *and this is really important*, I don't see these fans as freaks, as though they like to suffer and lose. At the end of the day, they are football fans and support their teams exactly the way I support mine, and some of you who are reading this book would probably do the same. They just happen to support a very small team.

A significant part of the project was to attend games, since watching football at the stadium is where the heart really pulses faster, a feeling that cannot be replicated on live TV. Travelling to watch football games live in the flesh – what a glamorous life! But no, not really. I had a very small budget to begin with, and the original publication in Portuguese was only possible after a successful crowdfunding. (What you're reading has been translated with small modifications. I have to thank Pitch Publishing for making it happen.) The book was the result of meticulous saving, planning, organisation and, of course, a crazy idea to throw caution to the wind.

Before and after the trip, I spent countless hours doing research, reading everything possible about these clubs, as I reached out to contacts across the globe. The entire concept – and I must say this again – is to write about fans and their experiences. I did not request press accreditations, but instead I wanted to watch the games where the regular people watch the games. Tracking these fans down was anything but easy, but a fundamental part of this project. The supporters are of different ages and social status, and might be part of ultras groups or not. The stories were written as told by the people, but I've included my personal observations. There was a considerable amount of research taken from newspapers, magazines, books and the Internet, and I conducted follow-up interviews with local journalists.

As this book was first published in Brazil in December 2017, some facts have changed since then (e.g., Queen's Park are no longer an amateur club, and Union Berlin now play in the Bundesliga) but I preferred not to alter the stories to reflect the sentiments of those fan bases at that particular time (sentiments that might persist even after aspects of their clubs did change).

I did not see any historic games. There were no celebration parades, or players signing multi-million contracts afterwards. These clubs are usually battling against relegation rather than chasing promotion or a title. However, what I've learned for sure is that nothing will stop these guys from supporting their teams. I went there to find out why. And hopefully you will enjoy what I uncovered.

CHAPTER 1

ESPANYOL AND THE WONDERFUL MINORITY

Real Madrid 2-0 Espanyol
Estadio Santiago Bernabéu
Saturday, 18 February 2017
La Liga (First Division)
Attendance: 72,234

The avenue was blocked for vehicles with barricades and mounted policemen. It is adjacent to the Santiago Bernabéu, and everyone wears a Real Madrid jersey, except for one person. On the pavement, amongst an ocean of white shirts, he seemed to know what nobody else there could: the bus that was about to appear in front of us was not bringing Cristiano Ronaldo, but a large blue coach with the less glamorous Espanyol players instead. Carlos Iglesias, 19, wearing a blue and white jersey with the number 21 on the back, raised his team's scarf above his head, and then put his fist in the air towards the bus, a powerful gesture.

People come from all over the world to see Real Madrid play, which makes the stadium's surrounding area full of tourists with no clue from where their team's bus will come.

Iglesias was not in Madrid to see the multi-champion *Galacticos*, but his beloved Espanyol from Barcelona. He lives in Salamanca, a two-hour trip from the capital, where he studies, and this is the first time he will watch an away game at Santiago Bernabéu. 'I'm here to support Espanyol and Espanyol only, but obviously Real Madrid is normally the team responsible for taking the league title away from them [FC Barcelona],' he says. 'I think that being an Espanyol fan is also being anti-Barça because they mistreat us. We need to celebrate when they suffer.'

Espanyol fans hate the big club of Barcelona almost more than they like their own. There is a widespread theory in football circles that Espanyol supporters represent an alliance with the Spanish monarchy (and Madrid) while the FC Barcelona fans are mostly Catalan separatists. Of course, RCD Espanyol's official name can be translated into English as 'Royal Spanish' and the club's crest is literally a crown, like many other clubs in Spain. However, this is not as simple and binary as it seems and many fans agree to disagree. Espanyol fans have two mantras.

The first mantra is that they support an apolitical football club. They claim that FC Barcelona use politics as a marketing tool, portraying Espanyol as the city villains. 'They are obviously a bigger club, but the problem is that our media in Catalonia is all about Barça, Barça and Barça,' Iglesias says. 'When it comes to Espanyol, they always have something negative to say, as if we are not a Catalan club. Barça is a very political club and everyone bought into their agenda.' Iglesias, nevertheless, believes that Catalonia is part of Spain.

Three hours before kick-off, I waited in front of Espanyol's hotel, a 15-minute walk from the stadium, to meet and greet some fans. There was not much action, but I was able to talk to a group of three students coming from a city outside of Madrid. They wore Espanyol jerseys and also carried a Spanish flag with them, even posing for a photo in front of the parked bus. The bus driver, Jose Manuel Martín, 49, himself a fanatic *perico* (the Espanyol fans' nickname, meaning parakeet), was also around smoking, a grey-haired man of few words. He was born and raised in Barcelona and he's firmly against Catalonia's independence from Spain.

If that was only a myth, all the Espanyol supporters that I came across up until that point proved the opposite. At the same time, this is an away game, at the epicentre of Spanish administration. These days in Barcelona there is a vocal group of pro-independence *pericos*. However, it is inconceivable for them to even be associated with FC Barcelona fans, even though some of them may share the separatist cause. They don't consider Barça fans as the spokesmen of the movement. Most supporters would not even admit that FC Barcelona is a local club. This is the second Espanyol fans' mantra right here: RCD Espanyol is the real Catalan club.

When I asked Martín, the grumpy bus driver, about this topic, he had a speech ready. 'Espanyol was founded by a Catalan student, while Barcelona was founded by a Swiss man with English players,' he says. 'We don't buy successful foreign players to win titles. They [Barcelona supporters] call us anti-Catalonia, but what do they really do for our community instead of just talk?' This is not as simple and binary as he says either, although he is correct about some FC Barcelona historical facts. It was founded by

Joan Gamper, a former player from FC Basel, Switzerland, from whom the club might have taken its iconic colours of blue and garnet (*blaugrana*) and the crest (the *balón*). The blue and white from Espanyol, on the other hand, are the colours appearing on the shield of a soldier from the Catalans' army.

In terms of historical players, FC Barcelona had László Kubala (Hungary), Johan Cruyff (Netherlands), Ronaldinho (Brazil) and Messi (Argentina). But when we think about Espanyol greats, everyone always has a Catalan player in mind. 'When you talk about Tamudo then you are talking about Espanyol and vice versa,' Carlos Iglesias says. The retired striker Raúl Tamudo holds the record for the most goals and appearances for Espanyol. He was not only born in Catalonia, but he is the Catalan-born footballer with the most goals scored in Spanish La Liga history with 146.

Tamudo and Espanyol were predestined for each other. He scored in his first professional game at the age of 19; he scored in two Copa del Rey Finals (a cup title ending 60 years of drought); he scored in all three stadiums that Espanyol has called home. And he scored a goal that made him revered by any *perico* supporter. *That goal he scored against Barça.*

Espanyol faced their local rivals at Camp Nou in June 2007, and with only two games left to play in the league, Real Madrid and FC Barcelona were level on points. Barça led Espanyol 2-1 after two goals scored by a 19-year-old Lionel Messi, while Real Madrid trailed Zaragoza away. Then in the 89th minute, Raúl Tamudo received a ball close to the FC Barcelona box and waited for the goalkeeper

Víctor Valdés to come out to meet him, so he could slip the ball home. Real Madrid eventually tied against Zaragoza and became champions in the final round. Raúl Tamudo's goal was ultimately what really sealed the deal. It has become known as *Tamudazo*.

The last-minute goal he scored against Barça was exactly what Tamudo needed to become Espanyol's top goalscorer in history. Every Espanyol supporter will tell this story as if it was an epic battle from the movie *Braveheart*. He became a legend not only for his accomplishments wearing the Espanyol jersey, but for taking FC Barcelona's league title away. Before I even asked, Carlos Inglesias told me why he supports a club that barely fights for big trophies.

'When you support a club in a city with a gigantic monster on your doorstep, you get to really appreciate the small victories,' he says. 'A goal like that one [against Barcelona] is perhaps not much when you support a team that wins the league every year, they [a Barça fan] would forget a week later. But for us that memory [of Tamudo's goal] is forever.' At the time I met Carlos, I didn't have a name for this book, but his speech about the giant stayed with me.

During the 1990s, Espanyol began using their motto *La força d'un sentiment* (The strength of a feeling) in their stadium's decor, marketing products and a documentary film released in 2011. The idea behind it was to show that their passion is not dependent on championships. They admit that their club is not as big as their rivals, but when Espanyol wins, it is always something special for them. Note: the slogan is in the Catalan language.

It always seems like Espanyol fans are fighting against their inferiority complex. A tourism campaign made by the regional government of Catalonia sparked a lot of controversy in 2016, after a promotional video ran with the tag line, 'If you feel FC Barcelona, you feel Catalunya'. *Los pericos* promptly launched a social media hashtag stating, 'We feel Samoa'. This is what they must deal with for supporting the other club from Barcelona: it's anything but easy.

Not long after that video aired, FC Barcelona beat Paris Saint-Germain 6-1 at home, which became a historical comeback in the UEFA Champions League (they lost the first leg 4-0). The president of *La Generalitat de Catalunya* (head of the regional government), Carles Puigdemont, would say that FC Barcelona's triumph was an inspiration in Catalonia's fight for independence. 'Nothing is impossible,' he wrote. 'Barça have just demonstrated this playing football. And Catalonia will demonstrate this by deciding its future,' he wrote in his Twitter account. In election campaigns, it is totally normal to see politicians wearing Barça jerseys, as if Espanyol voters did not exist.

The two largest sports newspapers from Barcelona, *Mundo Deportivo* and *Diario Sport*, respectively, dedicate an average of 25 of their pages each to FC Barcelona and no more than two pages to Espanyol, which is less than what they will devote to basketball coverage (also heavily focused on Barça I should mention). The message in the media is truly clear: Barcelona is not a football club within a city; it's more like a city within a football club.

More than their dynasty in football, FC Barcelona became a representation of Catalan culture, a community that preserves its own identity. However, pro-Catalonia symbolism was never a huge presence in the club before General Francisco Franco took over the country. The political divisiveness between Espanyol and Barça is a direct heritage of when the dictator ruled over Spain from 1939 to 1975. He took power after a bloody civil war, a conflict where Catalonia ended up defeated. The regime wanted national unity, so teaching Catalan in schools became illegal as did any public demonstration of the Catalan flag.

Franco's idea was to shut down any identification with Catalonia. His populist project used football as a platform to promote the country's strength (fascist propaganda at its best). He picked Real Madrid, the club from the capital, to give Europe a taste of his power. It is important to emphasise Franco was not a Real Madrid fan or even a football fan. It was all about his ideology.

FC Barcelona became then a symbol of resistance. Barça's Camp Nou stadium was a safe space for Catalan patriotic rebels, where people would come to express their political discontent, also forbidden during dictatorship. That is how FC Barcelona supporters' nationalism was born. It was not really only about football anymore. The club was not political for its first five decades, but this is how they are seen today. The civil war is a vivid memory in Spain and no football club wants to be attached to General Franco, even tenuously.

FC Barcelona fans routinely imply that Espanyol had a Franconian ideology and the club was favoured by the regime – an allegation also made against Real Madrid, especially after they won eight league titles in the 1960s. However, even if many Espanyol fans are pro-monarchy, the club had nothing to do with dictatorship. There is no time in history (before or after Franco) that Espanyol came close to competing with FC Barcelona in terms of results on the pitch.

In more than 70 years of La Liga history, Spain's national league, Espanyol finished above FC Barcelona in the table only three times. Even during Franco's darkest times, Barça managed to pull off a couple of national titles. Espanyol never won the league, not once, and the club's origin is actually largely connected with the city's hard working class. FC Barcelona, on the other hand, was always a rich club representing the city's elite. The inconvenient truth is that when General Franco died in 1975, FC Barcelona was, and still is, incredibly rich.

Espanyol fans really struggle with the Franco connection made by their rivals, which they claim is largely unfair. The club didn't take part in the war, and according to Espanyol fans, FC Barcelona used the dictatorship to reinforce their elite status in the city. Not only that, but the way their supporters see it, Espanyol was arguably a smaller club and they suddenly watched their biggest rivals 'steal' the Catalan identity from everybody else.

Nationalism and Catalan identity is a boomerang subject in the conversations I had. Espanyol fans have an urge to show the world that they are not anti-Catalan. Since 1995, the club has adopted a 'Catalanised' form of its official name, Reial Club Deportiu Espanyol de Barcelona (the word *deportiu* derives from the original word *deportivo* in Castilian). The club anthem and the stadium's announcements are in the Catalan language. *La força d'un sentiment* is Catalan.

The far-right ultra group *Brigadas Blanquiazules* (Blue-white brigades) with strong ties to anti-separatism, and pro-monarchy, pro-Spain and remarkably racist, were banned in the stadium for more than a decade. The group considers that spreading Catalan is a betrayal to the 'Espanyol roots'.

However, upon closer inspection, the yellow and red flags of Catalonia were seen at Estadio Sarrià for a long time (in the UEFA Cup Final that they lost in 1988, for example). According to Dutch sociologist Ramón Spaaij, 'Espanyol fan bases accuse FC Barcelona of exploiting their favourable social, economic and political position to recruit young talent from the region, driven by the ambition to overpower all the others, ultimately killing smaller clubs in Catalonia.'[1] It is a fair statement when you compare with clubs from the Madrid region, where several teams from the capital frequently play in Spain's first division (Getafe, Leganés, Rayo Vallecano). On the other hand, Catalonia has been basically Barça and Espanyol for a decade – an exception being Girona in the 2017/18 season, a club co-owned by Pere Guardiola (Pep's brother) and the City Football Group (owners of Manchester City). A third club from Barcelona, CE Europa, a historical founder member of La Liga, currently plays in the fourth division. Nobody remembers they exist unless you're a football fanatic.

All that being said, in case some of you are tracking whose club is 'more Catalan' than the other, during a *Derbi Barceloní* in 2017, Espanyol had three times more Catalan-born players on the pitch than Barça. Ironically, Espanyol's owner is a Chinese businessman, who, I could only assume, has no affiliation with this history (FC Barcelona, meanwhile, is an associative club and since 1978 their elected president has been born in the city).

Even if Espanyol was founded by students from

---

1 Spaaij,R., *Understanding Football Hooliganism: A Comparison of Six Western European Football Clubs.* (Amsterdam: Amsterdam University Press, 2006)

the University of Barcelona, at the same time the club suffers from its lack of *local* identity. Its current training facility is in Mina, on the outskirts of the city, and its ground at Cornellà-El Prat, the club's third stadium, is not even technically in the city. The fan favourite Sarrià stadium, a historical venue used in the 1982 World Cup, an area with the highest income per capita in Barcelona, was also a contrast to a historically working-class fan base. Montjuic, where they played after Sarrià was closed in 1997, is a pleasurable tourist area, but the stadium was a white elephant from the 1992 Summer Olympics, with an awful racing track separating the pitch and the crowd.

Barcelona has more than one club and Espanyol fans want you to know that. They have been playing in the first division for 25 consecutive years, and they are considerably bigger than other clubs in this book. Espanyol have won four Copa del Rey titles (2006 being the most recent), and played in two UEFA Cup Finals (both lost on penalty kicks). The club's average attendance is 20,000 per game, which is only small compared with the 80,000 from their rivals *blaugranas*. There is no Messi and co., so tourists are not lining up at the Espanyol stadium.

When Espanyol opened the Cornellà-El Prat in 2009, it was supposed to be the beginning of a new era for the club. The stadium is big, with a capacity of 40,000, modern and beautiful, but the reality proved different. A decade after its inauguration season, Espanyol's average attendance has been going down each season. Each game feels half-empty, with less attendance than smaller clubs like Málaga or Levante. The lack of transportation is an issue, but *perhaps*

Espanyol have only 20,000 fans willing to attend a game after all.

The concept of globalisation in football suits the big clubs perfectly, like FC Barcelona, and other European giants. Their games are on live TV in the United States, Indonesia and Singapore every week. It's even on live TV in Brazil, for God's sake! These clubs attract supporters worldwide because of their Ronaldos and Messis. But for smaller clubs with no superstars like RCD Espanyol, the Asian market is a distant reality. They are oceans apart.

A recent survey promoted by the Catalan government stated that Espanyol have only three per cent of fans in Barcelona. The city has more supporters of Real Madrid (ten per cent) than Espanyol fans. After the survey had been published, the club released a statement (again) by saying that 'no survey is necessary to understand that those three per cent are the most honoured'. The club and the Espanyol supporters started calling themselves *maravillosa minoría* (the wonderful minority).

When we compare Espanyol to FC Barcelona's popularity, the Camp Nou Museum was the most visited tourist site within Catalonia in 2016 (according to the Catalan Tourist Board). The museum had sold more entry tickets than the Picasso Museum or Gaudí's Casa Batlló. In fact, more people visited Barça's museum in that year than all of Espanyol's actual games.

The divisiveness between the two clubs is not social, political or religious. This is because every single category in the city has a *blaugrana* prevalence. Espanyol's resistance comes only from family tradition, not from a specific region, something passed from generation to generation.

Carlos Iglesias had to rely on his father's best friend to take him to his first Espanyol game. 'I felt like being part of a family, and after the game I could not explain my excitement,' he says.

I wanted to be part of this wonderful minority as well, so I sent an email to the club expressing my interest to buy a ticket for the away section at Santiago Bernabéu. The response was vague and bureaucratic. 'To buy tickets to attend the away visitors' area you have to be a member of Espanyol and buy them in our stadium,' they told me. The superclubs may be the villains of this book, but FC Barcelona would have handled that request differently, I'd assume. They wouldn't have wasted the opportunity to gain a new supporter (or *customer*, if you will).

Not entirely convinced, I persevered and just bought a ticket online for the fourth tier in the North End zone, close to where away supporters are concentrated at the Bernabéu. Only a handful of stewards separated both fan bases, and the ultras from Real Madrid stayed on the other side of the stadium. It was just like being an away fan. Mission accomplished.

Away fans is not a huge tradition in Spain as it is in Germany or England. I was not surprised that less than 100 Espanyol fans turned up, but disappointed nonetheless. The pre-match experience outside was non-existent: no chants, no pints, no greasy street food. I approached several *pericos* close to the entrance gates, but none of them made the trip from Barcelona exclusively to watch the game – they were mostly Madrid residents. The away section inside wasn't any different, as it could have easily been mistaken for a John Mayer concert.

Real Madrid fans were no more enthusiastic though. The *merengues* crowd is not exactly famous for being noisy, and everything felt a bit theatrical like a ballet performance, with an intense celebration only after goalscoring. The atmosphere is definitely different from South American stadiums (and by this I mean much worse). Real Madrid's Ultras Sur are probably the most awkward ultra group in Europe, with the average crowd being more interested in taking a Cristiano Ronaldo snapshot than watching the game. Tourists are visible everywhere (and of course, I don't exclude myself from this category). The Bernabéu has a history and mystique, but the whole experience is really flat compared to what I'm used to.

I spoke to a supporters' club member of the *Penya Espanyolista* of Madrid, an organised Espanyol fan club living in the city. There are advantages of living apart from their team, he concluded. 'We're not as exposed to the Barcelona media and the government celebrating Barça all the time. It is the opposite here [in Madrid] because all the newspapers have nothing good to say about Barça,' he laughs. 'The Catalan press only remembers that we exist when Espanyol is taking on Real Madrid and they need us to win. It's like magic.'

He is not far from reality in this case. *Mundo Deportivo*'s columnist Tarzán Migueli, an iconic Barcelona defender who played 20 seasons for the club, once wrote that if Espanyol was not in the league, Real Madrid would have six less points in the table. Which is not exactly accurate according to the numbers provided by the journalist Pedro Martin. 'Espanyol has earned 109 points against Barcelona and 111 against Real Madrid in the league's history,' he writes.

This is the only away game I attended in a different city for this book, essentially because many Barça fans believe that Espanyol don't play hard enough against Real Madrid. I've seen Espanyol play at the Cornellà Stadium on a different occasion, so I took this game in Madrid as an opportunity to understand the alleged alliance. To get a sense of whether there was a political brotherhood in place, both clubs being named Real, and whether they are (allegedly) pro-monarchy.

Before the match, I asked fans if they supported both Espanyol and Real Madrid, but I couldn't really feel a true fraternity (the exception being a military man I talked to in front of the hotel, who confessed supporting both teams equally). At least for those fans I spoke with, it seemed like their connection to Real Madrid is mainly because they can beat FC Barcelona. As one might say, if Barça played against a dog, an Espanyol fan would start barking.

In the 2015/16 season, Real Madrid beat Espanyol twice with the score of 6-0 (including the infamous game where Cristiano Ronaldo scored five goals). In fact, before the kick-off Espanyol hadn't beaten Real Madrid for more than 20 matches, and nothing changed that afternoon. Gareth Bale and Álvaro Morata scored one apiece, and Real Madrid won 2-0 in front of a crowd that celebrated a Ronaldo elastico nutmeg against a defender more frenetically than the goals. Espanyol had zero shots on target and their fans quietly left before the final whistle.

While it is true that Espanyol cannot beat Real Madrid, it is also true that they cannot beat FC Barcelona (like almost every team in Spanish football). Espanyol never beat Barça in the league playing in their new-*ish* Cornellà

Stadium; their last victory at home was in 2007, under head coach Ernesto Valverde (who went on to become the FC Barcelona coach). Espanyol's last derby victory at Camp Nou was more than ten years ago, under head coach Mauricio Pochettino, an Espanyol favourite who once declared he will never coach FC Barcelona.

After I concluded all the travelling for this book, I came to the conclusion that Espanyol fans are the ones with the most resentment towards their local rivals. Apart from their individual political beliefs, what really brings Espanyol fans together is their aversion to FC Barcelona. The club once faced disciplinary action after their fans raised a banner that read *Shakira es de todos* (Shakira is everyone's), since the singer is married to Gerard Piqué. (The Barça defender scored a late goal against Espanyol in 2018, and celebrated in front of their fans holding his finger to his lips; the goal sealed a record-breaking unbeaten league run for Barcelona.)

Espanyol fans also frequently carry a banner that says, *Catalunya es mes que un club* (Catalonia is more than one club) to antagonise FC Barcelona's famous slogan *Més que un club* (More than a club). Later in the 2016/17 season, amid local unrest, Barça requested a game be postponed after a Catalonia independence referendum was rejected by the authorities. La Liga denied their request and threatened to punish the club by taking away six points, and FC Barcelona eventually played behind closed doors instead 'as a protest'. This is what makes Espanyol fans consider them to be hypocrites. According to them, if FC Barcelona were really 'more than a club', they would support the Catalan demonstration for independence at all costs. At the end of the day, it proved itself to be just a football club.

Another symbol of the strong Espanyol link to Catalonia was the defender Dani Jarque, who started playing for the club in the youth system and appeared in more than 250 professional games. In 2009, Jarque became the team's captain in the Cornellà-El Prat Stadium inauguration, but he was found dead a week later during Espanyol's pre-season in Florence, due to a heart attack. He was 26 years old and left behind his girlfriend who was seven months pregnant. He is not only a symbol, but a martyr for the *pericos*.

Espanyol fans stand up and clap every game in the 21st minute, Jarque's jersey number. Gate 21 at Cornellà is a must-visit sanctuary with pictures, flowers and scarves. The T-shirt worn by Andrés Iniesta under his Spanish jersey in the 2012 World Cup Final is on display there – Iniesta scored the winning goal, and ran towards the cameras showing that exact same T-shirt with the words *Dani Jarque siempre con nosotros* (Dani Jarque forever with us). For all the hatred that Espanyol fans feel for what FC Barcelona represents, an incredibly touching gesture came from a Barça player (Iniesta and Jarque played together for Spain's youth teams).

With all that in mind, I knew the significance of the number 21, right there in front of me before kick-off, on the pavement close to the Santiago Bernabéu. 'Dani Jarque gave his life for this club, literally and metaphorically,' Carlos Iglesias says, wearing Jarque's jersey. 'He gave everything he had, for every game he played. He represented our sentiment on the pitch, and if it was up to me to decide, nobody would ever wear the number 21 again. It should at least be worn only by a homegrown player just like him. The number 21 is sacred for us.'

Iglesias couldn't enjoy a better result visiting Madrid for the first time, but he had nonetheless a good football experience with his older brother. 'What is your biggest dream for Espanyol?' I ended up asking. 'I wish we could win a European trophy,' he says. 'We lost two [UEFA Cup] finals in the past on penalty kicks, so I reckon that it would be possible for us to win it one day.' However, what I really wanted to know was an *impossible* dream. 'Oh, if we're talking about a crazy, crazy, crazy dream, then *it has to be* winning the league against Barcelona, that is for sure,' he confesses.

Well, that is unlikely to happen soon (if ever). It has been a long time since the *Tamudazo* goal, but when Espanyol visited the Santiago Bernabéu on that Saturday afternoon, once again Real Madrid and Barcelona were battling for the league title, like they always do. Espanyol showed no resistance to Real Madrid, another casual help for the enemy's enemy. Three months later, Real Madrid won La Liga and the UEFA Champions League. Not ideal for the Espanyol fans, but good enough to keep their anti-Barça sentiment alive.

Next stop: Vallecas, Madrid
Distance: 5km (3 miles) from Metro Puerta del Sol
How to get there: 25 minutes by Metro
The best advice: Grab a *bocadillo de jamón* and a San Miguel beer, and enjoy the day.
Soundtrack: 'Mala Vida' by Mano Negra

CHAPTER 2

LOVE RAYO, HATE RACISM

Rayo Vallecano 1-2 Mirandés
Campo de Fútbol de Vallecas
Sunday, 19 February 2017
La Liga 2 (Second Division)
Attendance: 8,567

The tourists who walked by the thousands in Puerta del Sol, Madrid's most famous and most central square, disappeared as I made my way to the Vallecas district. There were no football fans in sight at the Metro station. There was not a single indication of the football game taking place in a couple of hours. Rayo Vallecano would soon take on Mirandés with both teams in the relegation zone of the second division. Not exactly a tourist attraction that people write about in travel guides.

I was thinking of a hypothetical *Who Wants To Be a Millionaire?* final question. 'What football team from Madrid wears a white jersey with a red diagonal stripe?' That's it! All someone needs to win a million pounds is to answer that question correctly. Real Madrid would be the easiest choice if one doesn't follow soccer whatsoever.

They're always in the news, between viral videos and a BuzzFeed quiz. Perhaps one would think that the answer to win the jackpot would not be so easy, right? What about Atlético Madrid then? They play in red and white colours, they are kinda known, but not as well as Real. Football fanatics think of such things as obvious, but it is really not. If you know Rayo Vallecano, a local neighbourhood club from Spain, then you are part of a small niche circle. Yeah, we all could be millionaires!

I was thinking about that on the train, before I got off at Metro Portazgo, 40 minutes south of the Santiago Bernabéu. Upon leaving the station, the Vallecas stadium is the first building you will see. Cristián González, 32, and Sergio Candel, 36, were waiting. Sergio is 6ft tall, with a huge beard, wears an ear gauge, a nose piercing, sunglasses and a beret. Cristián is 5ft 8in, wearing jeans and the club's jersey – a more traditional guy. They immediately gave me a Rayo Vallecano scarf as a gift. Then we headed off to the closest bar. 'For us, this is what it is all about, meeting up with friends, having a beer, and laughing when you can while supporting Rayo,' says Sergio. 'We can't always expect to win the game.'

The two friends met at the University of Alcalá in a city 35km north-east of Madrid. What were the odds? Two Rayo Vallecano supporters studying in the same programme, in the same classroom, and never bumped into each other in the stadium? It wouldn't be that surprising if they supported a big team, but Vallecas is a very small stadium, and the overwhelming majority of the Rayo fans live in the neighbourhood (that is probably why I saw no supporters on the Metro). Rayo Vallecano is, in fact, one of the last true neighbourhood teams in Spain (or Europe). To better understand the culture of the club, it is necessary to understand the place itself. Because Rayo is Vallecas and Vallecas is Rayo.

The two districts of Vallecas in Madrid (Puente de Vallecas, which is the larger, where the stadium is located, and the smaller Villa de Vallecas) together have a population of 300,000. A rental place to live in this area is almost half of the price you'd pay for a place in Chamartín, the Santiago Bernabéu area. It is an area of housing estates and considered one of the poorest parts of the city (it is not in extreme poverty, but definitely a visibly working-class area).

Incorporated into greater Madrid in the 1950s, Vallecas has been a place for historical battles for basic rights, such as getting electricity and properly treated water. It has also been an entry point to the capital for Spanish migrants, and more recently, immigrants. In 2016, according to the city's records, it was the district with the highest unemployment rate in Madrid. Consequently, Vallecas has been affected by an increase in organised crime and violence. The residents always felt like they were left to their own devices and only local social movements prioritised the neighbourhood, which explains why Rayo Vallecano fans increasingly forged an association with left-wing politics, which was quick to rally for their causes.

Puente de Vallecas is to this day the only district in Madrid that has never elected a congressman from the most conservative Partido Popular (People's Party). The club's identity as left-wing is an extension of its fans (who live and work there), and not the other way around. Protesting is in the neighbourhood's DNA and when I got there, Rayo Vallecano was in the middle of turmoil. Their fans decided they had had enough of its owner. As soon as we finished a couple of bottled beers, Cristián, Sergio and I joined a demonstration.

The street rally and fan march took in several side streets and finished in front of the club's locker room an hour before kick-off. It is literally a door with access to a corner street. Even before the demonstration, I'd seen hundreds of stickers around the stadium printed *Presa Vete Ya* (Presa leave now), with the club owner's picture photoshopped with Mickey Mouse ears. Raul Martín Presa took over in 2011 when he bought the club for €900 – that's right, nine hundred euros – regulated by the Spanish Insolvency Act (he technically took on the club's debts). It was great timing, as Rayo Vallecano had been recently promoted to the first division.

With its new chairman in charge, Rayo Vallecano played five consecutive years in the Spanish elite, which is a club record. They finished eighth in the 2012/13 season, the club's highest position in its history. If we were only to analyse the results on the pitch, it was far from a disaster, even when Rayo Vallecano was eventually relegated back to the second division in 2016. However, there is a fundamental truth that you need to understand when talking about Rayo Vallecano supporters: it is not only about the results on the pitch.

During this particular protest, the fans chanted against Martín Presa and raised banners against him. An ultra leader from the *Bukaneros* used a megaphone to prompt several choruses and accuse the chairman of corruption. Cristián, who was very outspoken about Rayo's history, tried to sum up the scenario. 'Our stadium is old and is not being repaired. Our youth team has been pushed aside for years because of a policy of hiring questionable players from elsewhere and the club's employees are not being paid,' he says. 'There are several contracts made with the owner's brother's company [Alfonso Presa] that should be investigated. There is no transparency or dialogue. Why in the world do we need to make business deals in Oklahoma, when he's not even taking care of our team right here?'

In August 2015, Martín Presa unsuccessfully purchased a team from Oklahoma City and renamed the club Rayo OKC; however, it folded after a year following a dispute between the co-owners. Rayo Vallecano fans felt like they didn't need a 'global expansion', since their greatest attribute is precisely the club's local aspect, which they felt had been abandoned. Rayo Vallecano supporters, more than other fans I've been in contact with, feel like they are part of the club. In some ways I would even say they feel like they *are* the club.

When it comes to support, Rayo Vallecano fans play their part with no hesitation. Following the relegation game in May 2016, a victory at home that ended up not being enough to save them, the fans chanted for their players for more than ten minutes, recognising their effort. When the club's owner suggested closing operations of Rayo Vallecano's women's side, a three-time Spanish champion (by far Rayo Vallecano's greatest achievement on the pitch), the fans themselves crowdfunded the necessary budget to acquire the licence for the team to play in the league. Ironically, Rayo Vallecano had the first woman president of an elite club in 1994.

The supporters often go beyond football, like when they raised banners in the stadium against the eviction of an 85-year-old Vallecas resident, Carmen Ayudo, during Spain's economic crisis in 2013. She was evicted from her house after living there since the 1960s due to the lack of a security loan payment. The fans' mobilisation eventually caught the attention of head coach Paco Jémez and the players, who then committed to paying her rent for the rest of her life. The story made international news, but this was not a global expansion. Rayo fans really care.

During Spain's now infamous general strike of 2012, the *Bukaneros* ultras (the buccaneers) even suggested Rayo Vallecano players stay home. On top of their political messages, the ultras are strongly against the commercialis-ation of football. When a game for the first division was scheduled for 10pm on a weekday, they protested, leaving their stands empty. Banners criticising ticket prices and La Liga's president, Javier Tebas, are quite common.

All that being said, the supporters' fury against the club's chairman was not only a matter of bad results on the pitch, even though Rayo Vallecano was fighting against relegation to the third division. To be associated with a right-wing fascist footballer was not something that the fans would allow. In a bar right in front of the stadium, a huge banner read, *por un barrio con nuestros simbolos* (for a neighbourhood with our values).

One week before my arrival in Madrid, Rayo Vallecano signed Ukranian midfielder Roman Zozulya from Sevilla's Real Betis. The *Bukaneros* released a manifesto showing the player's alleged links to the Azov Battalion, a neo-Nazi movement in his home country. That would be intolerable for any club, but especially for one with a mural inside its grounds that says, *Ama Al Rayo, Odia El Racismo* (Love Rayo, Hate Racism). The mural has an image of former English international Laurie Cunningham, who ended his career with the club before he was tragically killed in a car crash (more about Cunningham later in this book).

When I contacted the *Bukaneros* for an interview, they sent me a dossier against Zozulya, in addition to an official statement, here translated from Spanish.

> *The entire world of football knows of our fans, and of our commitment to our neighbourhood, our demonstrations against racism and homophobia. This is the result of years of work and awareness in the stands of Vallecas [stadium]. The arrival of this player, what he represents and his ideas, would be a contradiction to what Rayo Vallecano means to all of us. Our striped jersey will not be stained.*

Roman Zozulya denied all the accusations against him, although he is seen in several photographs wearing the white supremacists group uniform, while saluting a 14/88 scoreboard on a basketball court – the 14-word slogan derived from *Mein Kampf,* and the eighth letter of the alphabet, a secret code to Heil Hitler. Following the negative backlash, Martín Presa backed down and cancelled the Ukrainian player's contract. He accused the *Bukaneros* of being leftie extremist radicals, which, to some extent, is not exactly untrue.

The demonstration I took part in before Rayo's game, however, was not from a specific group of fans. 'They always accuse us of making politics and being intolerant,' says Cristián, who is a regular fan, and not part of the *Bukaneros*. 'Not accepting a Nazi player in our club goes beyond any political or ideological causes that one might support. This is the very least we can do as a society. You cannot separate football from daily life and if today we accept a Nazi footballer, there will be a day where we will accept a Nazi prime minister.'

When I told Cristián that I'd be going to St. Pauli the following week, he confessed that the Hamburg club is an inspiration because of both their left-wing politics and the club's neighbourhood roots. He thinks Rayo Vallecano should be globally recognised for being Antifa, just like St. Pauli. They don't have a romanticised idea about themselves. Rayo Vallecano is really a small neighbourhood club. They are no bigger than, let's say, Leyton Orient in London.

The following week when I was in Hamburg, perhaps not by coincidence, the St. Pauli ultras raised a banner at *Millerntor-Stadion* in support of Rayo Vallecano fans and against the allegedly Nazi footballer. The banner carried a message in Spanish reading, *Con Nazis no se Juega, Aupa Rayo!* (We don't play with Nazis. Be strong Rayo!) I sent a photo to Cristián that in a few minutes was spread all over *Bukaneros's* social media.

However, following the Zozulya incident, La Liga officials ended up forbidding a dozen of Rayo Vallecano fans attending games for the rest of the season. All fans spent the entire match against Mirandés chanting effusively against Martín Presa and Javier Tebas. *No queremos ver cómo hundes al Rayo, escucha al aficionado, ¡Presa márchate!* (We don't want to see our Rayo sink. Listen to the fans,

41

Presa you must leave!) said one chant. Unfortunately, he wouldn't leave. The fans did not heckle their players, not even after the team lost the game.

The atmosphere at Vallecas is worth every penny, almost like travelling in time. It has terraces and the fans behind the goal can stand for the whole game. The stadium's toilet are like a movie set from the 1960s: crappy and falling apart. Not to mention the fact that one of the goal ends does not have a grandstand, just a big wall with red and white panels covered with the words *valentia, coraje y nobleza* (bravery, courage and nobility). The ambience is fantastic and noisy all the time, a non-league football vibe with players a few metres away, or a simulacrum of Argentine fans (coincidentally Rayo Vallecano adopted their distinctive red sash in 1949 after receiving shirts from Argentina's River Plate, that were in Madrid to face Real Madrid).

Whether the quality of the game was inversely proportional to what I'd seen a day before at the Bernabéu, the same can be said about the two fan bases. Rayo Vallecano fans participate; it is not like a Real Madrid theatre. The fans are immersed in politics, but care a lot about football. On my side, the bearded Sergio whined all the time about his team's performance. 'I think it will be hard to score a goal if we don't shoot a ball on target,' he grumbles, following the 0-0 scoreline at half-time. However, Rayo Vallecano quickly scored in the opening of the second half, the ball finding the net right in front of us, as the players celebrated steps away from us.

Sergio had warned me before the game, though, that one can't have fun and expect Rayo Vallecano to win at the same time. Mirandés drew level and then scored the come-from-behind goal with only five minutes to play. Rayo Vallecano's head coach was fired after the game and was replaced by Míchel, the club's top goalscorer (a decision that the fans agreed upon). 'If I became ill every time Rayo didn't win a game, I would be dead already,' Sergio says. 'It is common for football fans to see football as a matter of life and death, but for us it is only part of our life really. All said and done, I have more joy than disappointments when supporting Rayo.'

Sergio was there when Rayo Vallecano made their international debut in the 2000/01 UEFA Cup, after qualifying through a Fair Play ranking. He went to the neighbouring country Andorra to see a 10-0 victory, the biggest in the club's history (more about Andorra later in this book). And Sergio was there when Rayo Vallecano was relegated to the third division, only three seasons later.

The small glories are the ones that the supporters share with pride. Such as when Rayo Vallecano beat Real Madrid away in 1996 (the first and only time); and a year later when they beat the Madrid giants again at Vallecas to end Fabio Capello's unbeaten run of 29 games (Real Madrid ended up winning the league). It was the last time that Rayo Vallecano won the local 'derby'. Back then it was easier for a neighbourhood club to pull off such miracles when football was not dependent on money.

During the club's debut season in the first division in 1978, Rayo Vallecano got a reputation for raising their game against the big clubs. They beat Real Madrid, Barcelona, Atlético Madrid, Valencia and Athletic Bilbao (the five biggest clubs in the country) and earned the nickname *Matagigantes* (giant-killers). That is not remotely possible anymore. During Rayo Vallecano's most recent stint in the elite, between 2012 and 2016, they lost ten of their games against Real Madrid, scoring nine goals in such matches, while Cristiano Ronaldo alone scored 12. Ronaldo's wages from Real Madrid (not to mention his endorsement deals) would cover Rayo Vallecano's payroll for three years. In today's football, a bag of money scores goals.

Rayo Vallecano, despite all their social involvement with the community, has always been a quirky club. Teresa Rivero stayed in charge for 17 years as the first female president of a football club, only named by her controversial businessman husband José Maria Ruiz-Mateos, who had spent a couple of years in jail for fraud and tax evasion before buying the club (he was also a member of religious institution Opus Dei). Rivero was an important figure to several Rayo fans, but his spouse's corruption and eventual new arrest in 2012 was what led the club to insolvency in the first place, leaving the door open for Martín Presa.

There is an idiosyncrasy in what the fans consider to be real football. The fans clamour for better facilities, but they don't want to risk losing the stadium's identity. They want to play in Spain's first division, but they are against the television schedule monopoly. They want better players, but it has to be better players who are socially conscious. It all seems to be fair, but it is a contradiction to the way modern football is ruled and fuelled by money. The bigger the economic gap, the more fans like Cristián and Sergio support movements like Against Modern Football. 'I went to the Bernabéu to see a Real Madrid game with a couple of friends and they won 6-1,' Cristián says. 'And people were complaining – can you believe that? I was there looking at them clueless. This is not really supporting your football team. Real Madrid fans chant about how they love their team because they won *la decima* [tenth UCL title]. So if they didn't win titles, their fans would stop loving the team?'

(It was clearly a rhetorical question, so I declined to answer. To be honest this is just football chants really. It doesn't mean anything. Rayo Vallecano fans also chant all the time about 'winning the league this year', something that clearly they won't do.)

Rayo Vallecano's results on the pitch also became unpredictable during their relative success in the first division. Under head coach Paco Jémez, the team used to play offensive football, refusing to park the bus, and more willing to take risks. However, it is hard to take risks in a league with FC Barcelona and Real Madrid. Rayo Vallecano lost 7-0 to Barça at home in 2012, the club's worst defeat ever at Vallecas. Three years later, they lost 10-2 to Real Madrid at the Bernabéu. 'Although you cannot forget that they [Real Madrid] played with 12 players against nine,' Cristián says, confidently. Rayo Vallecano led 2-1 before the referee, the 12th Real Madrid player on the pitch, according to Cristián, sent off two of the Rayo players even before half-time (blaming the referee for a 10-2 loss – what self-confidence!).

The supporters are not immune to a change of political views in their neighbourhood, which would become the ultimate idiosyncrasy for the club. People have changed, politicians have changed and the Vallecas neighbourhood might change. What would happen if a leftie working-class population became more conservative, sparked by anti-immigration populists? It could be a significant loss for the *barrio*. Would the Rayo Vallecano fans follow such a trend?

It would be especially traumatic for *rayistas*, since they are literally the first Spanish club to give voice in the fight against racism. The Nigerian goalkeeper Wilfred 'Willy' Agbonavbare is one of Rayo Vallecano's favourite players. He played six years for the club after reporting for training in 1990, unemployed, looking for an opportunity. 'The neighbourhood was different back then, and you didn't see as many black people in the streets,' Cristián says. 'I can't imagine what he had to go through when it comes to racism in Madrid. More than a good goalkeeper, we consider Willy a Rayo Vallecano hero.' On the wall of the main gate at Vallecas stadium, there is a big mural of the goalie that says, *Eterno Willy*.

Spain is not exactly known for its lack of racism on the terraces, most notably in the 1980s and 1990s. A shocking news report from 1992 aired on TV significantly captures the overt racism launched at Willy from the Real Madrid fans, as they continued to shout: *Negro, cabrón, recoge al algodón* (Negro, asshole, go pick cotton). Real Madrid fans openly talked to a reporter before the kick-off saying that the Nigerian goalkeeper should go back to Africa.

Thirty years ago social movements were not vocally active yet, and when interviewed, an embarrassed Willy responded by saying that 'this is just part of football'. Not for Rayo Vallecano fans – that is definitely not part of football. Willy played over 150 matches for the club, in addition to the 1994 World Cup when he was called up as Nigeria's backup keeper. He worked as a luggage assistant at the Baracas airport following his retirement and died of cancer in 2015 at the tender age of 48. Willy allegedly sent all of his footballer money to his wife who still lived in Nigeria. Wilfred Agbonavbare was buried with a Rayo Vallecano flag on his coffin.

A couple of years ago, Rayo Vallecano also introduced an anti-homophobia jersey with a rainbow stripe instead of its traditional red one. The club always brings awareness to honourable causes. They had a pink-stripe jersey to honour the fight against cancer. It could be perceived as opportunistic marketing, 'global expansion', or as 'woke' behaviour, but it has credibility coming from Rayo Vallecano.

And despite all the *barrio* mythology surrounding the club, Vallecas has a big Real Madrid fan base, since it is the largest district in Madrid (it is larger than the city of Bilbao, for instance), and has a high concentration of immigrants, which tends to associate itself with the most successful clubs. 'There are some people who come to the stadium every [Rayo Vallecano] game, but they support Real Madrid instead,' says Sergio. 'When we play against Madrid, it is always the biggest game of the season for us.' Real Madrid has fans everywhere in the world. It goes pretty much like this: every Rayo Vallecano fan is from Vallecas, but not everyone from Vallecas is a Rayo Vallecano fan.

Around the stadium everything is evidently related to the club: bars, kebab houses, corner stores, almost every commercial building has a red lightning bolt for Rayo. The most important thing, according to Sergio, is that the Vallecas stadium remains a community area, a place in the neighbourhood to watch professional football and, with any luck, enough local people will support their small team that won't win major titles. Just like they say in one of those Rayo Vallecano chants: 'it doesn't matter if we never win; our red stripe is the most sacred'.

When it comes to Atlético Madrid, the other big club in the city, their fan base is concentrated mostly in the southern part of the city. It is normally associated with a 'working-class' fan base, which Cristián strongly disagrees with. 'They are working class only if you compare them to Real Madrid,' he says. 'Their ultras Frente Atletico is one of the most fascist in all Spain. Would you call that working class?' In 2019, the group displayed several racist banners in Vallecas, including Confederate flags. Obviously, I'm not here to make generalisations, but when I walked around Atlético's stadium Vicente Calderón, it was not hard to find right-wing graffiti (in 2017 Atlético moved across the city to one of the richest areas at Wanda Metropolitano).

The most central and touristy areas in Madrid are all in Real Madrid territory (the club has three megastores at Grand Vía, Madrid's main shopping avenue). On the contrary, Rayo Vallecano merchandising is just impossible to find anywhere outside their stadium (and they ship only within Spain). During matchdays, street vendors stay only until kick-off. A Rayo Vallecano fan is also hard to find outside the Vallecas neighbourhood. I saw a morning jogger wearing the club's jacket at iconic Parque del Retiro, and I even thought about asking him some questions about supporting the club but a) I'm not a complete creep; and b) he was running really fast.

After the loss against Mirandés, some fans gathered in front of the locker rooms, the same door we all protested against the club's owner outside a couple of hours before the game. However, this time they were there to give Rayo Vallecano players a final word of support in the club's battle against relegation, which they eventually escaped from, after the club's idol Míchel took charge as head coach. Rayo Vallecano is not in the shadow of a giant, as they are smaller than a shadow. 'Small on the pitch, but big when it comes to our values', as the fans' mantra says.

On my way home, Sergio and Cristián told me about Cerro del Tío Pío, a mountain in Vallecas with the best view of Madrid, according to them, and also affectionately known by the locals as *Parque de las Siete Tetas*, which roughly translates to Park of the Seven Tits (and is an accurate description). At the top, after a beautiful Sunday of football, looking at the Madrid sunset in silence, I gazed upon the entire city from a distance as a red lightning bolt flashed across the horizon. Okay, the lightning part is not true. But it would have been beautiful.

Next stop: Munich, Germany
Distance: 1,960km (1,218 miles)
How to get there: Two hours and 40 minutes by plane
The best advice: Learn the difference between S-Bahn and U-Bahn, and pray for the best
Soundtrack: 'El vals del Obrero' by Ska-P

CHAPTER 3

THE INCREDIBLE FAILURE OF 1860 MUNICH

TSV 1860 2-0 Nürnberg
Allianz Arena
Monday, 20 February 2017
2. Bundesliga (Second Division)
Attendance: 24,100

I had met a variety of random people from Bavaria before even visiting Munich for the first time. So this particular story begins 15 years ago, in Porto Alegre, Brazil, when two German exchange students stayed at my best friend's girlfriend's house. We took them to an Internacional regional summer league game at Beira-Rio Stadium where they spent the entire match sunbathing on the terraces. Two years later, during a road trip I made along the Brazilian coast, in the city of Natal I met this girl from Ausgburg, Bavaria, who supported Bayern. A few days later, in Recife, I met this fella from Regensburg, Bavaria, who also supported Bayern. Eventually I moved to Canada where I worked with this kid from a small village called Weilheim, 50km south of Munich (exactly the same place where Thomas Müller was born), and guess what? Every time I asked Bavarian people about the other team in Munich, the answer was the same: 'Nobody supports 1860 in Munich.'

An attendance of 24,000 is far from nobody, I thought, as I took my seat on that freezing Monday night to watch the match. 1860 Munich faced FC Nürnberg in a Bavarian derby and the atmosphere was even frostier. At the time the club was playing its games at the Allianz Arena, and after five consecutive years in the second division, they had the worst occupancy rate of the entire league (close to 34 per cent, meaning the stadium is always two-thirds empty). They never exceeded the average of 25,000 fans per game in a single season, compared to the city's giants Bayern who have sold out to a crowd of 75,000 fans for all of their games in the Bundesliga.

Unlike Bayern Munich games, which are very hard to find tickets for (unless you buy them from a travel agency as part of an overpriced package), for the 1860 Munich game I just showed up at the box office a couple of hours before kick-off. The cheapest tickets are for the standing sectors behind the goals; these spots are truly a German tradition. The North Curve at the stadium (*Nordkurve*) is reserved for the 1860 Munich ultras while the South Curve (*Südkurve*) is for Bayern's ultras when their team plays there. The standing sector was sold out, so I just bought a regular ticket for €15 and stood up regardless as the stadium was semi-empty.

However, first I needed to do what every German would do before a game: *bier und currywurst*. It was my third game in three consecutive nights and I had woken up at 4am to catch a flight that morning (something I don't recommend after a certain age). It was also not my smartest decision to underestimate the weather, as I wore only a hoodie with no gloves. I know, it seems like a typical Brazilian rookie mistake, but hear me out: compared to the milder Madrid temperature I was experiencing only a day earlier, 4°C in Munich feels like it is Siberia.

The stadium's location is not exactly the most pleasant either: a huge open field with nothing around it and the temperature can feel much colder because of the wind. Further away from downtown, in the suburban area of Fröttmaning, the area seemed more fitting for an airport or a maximum security prison, but they built this luxurious sports facility instead. On the other hand, the stadium is easily accessible by public transport (like almost all in Munich), even if it entails a good 15-minute walk from the nearest U-Bahn station.

Upon leaving the station, the stadium catches your eye immediately. It is a must-see for every football fanatic, especially on game nights, due to its magnificent lighting, in the colours of red for Bayern games, blue for 1860 Munich, or white for the German national team. The police were out in huge numbers around the stadium, specifically mounted police. FC Nürnberg ultras are not exactly lords and gentlemen and they tried to break security turnstiles before the horses were put there to block them from doing so. On that evening, it was more like a scuffle than proper violence, and bottles flew around the place like carnival confetti.

Shortly after I arrived, I met Luis Lessner, 22, a university student, and his retired father, Christian, 54, two

1860 Munich fans travelling from Nürnberg (of all places!). They have been supporting the team since forever, for generations really. 'As for me, it's like I was born a fan, with a mix of family tradition and love for the club,' Luis says. 'I have the heart of a lion and I would never change what was passed down to me from my father and grandfather. This is important for all fans I believe, knowing that winning is not what matters the most.'

The club's nickname amongst the supporters is The Lions (*Die Lowen*), and its official name, TSV München von 1860, means Gymnastic and Sport Club Munich from 1860. Although, like most supporters, Luis refers to the club only as *Sechzig* (60 in German). The fan base is largely related to a family tradition more than necessarily coming from a specific area in Munich. Also, like most *Sechzig* supporters, Luis hates that they have to play at the Allianz Arena.

Bayern Munich has been the stadium's sole owner since 2006, when 1860 Munich sold 50 per cent of its shares to pay off debts, basically meaning that *Sechzig* paid rent to their biggest rival. Not only that, everything inside the big stadium reminds them of Bayern: the red colours on the walls, the big panels with pictures of Bayern's players, their megastore, which smartly enough is closed during 1860 Munich games. The 1860 apparel and merchandising is sold through small kiosks, similar to those used by hot dog vendors. Nothing at the Allianz Arena feels like their home whatsoever, with the exception of the astonishing blue lighting.

The ground-sharing with Bayern was a daydream from Karl-Heinz Wildmoser, the club's former president from

1992 to 2004. 1860 Munich had just finished fourth in the 1999/2000 Bundesliga season and the club was set to play in the UEFA Champions League the next season (where they were eventually eliminated by Leeds United). It was a *Cinderella* story that fell short of a happy ending, and everything since then fell apart.

Wildmoser and his son were arrested in March 2004 on charges of taking bribes from a construction company that built the arena for the 2006 World Cup (the former president passed away in 2010). In May 2004, after a decade in Germany's top flight, 1860 Munich were relegated to the second division and never came back. The stadium turned out to be too big and expensive for a second-tier side to be built. They sold their interest in the arena in April 2006. The club never played a single Bundesliga match at the Allianz Arena.

1860 Munich managed to sell out the stadium only a handful of times. A 25-year-old fan who prefers to go by the nickname Giko, and lives in a village with a population of 3,000 situated an hour south of Munich, remembers one of these games, against Borussia Dortmund in 2013. 'I was in the *Nordkurve* and there is a big supporter friendship between Dortmund and 1860 and the atmosphere was insane,' he says. 'We [1860] managed to get into overtime, when we then sadly lost, but I never left a game where we lost this happy before or ever again.' Both fan bases sing 'You'll Never Walk Alone' before the matches, and they both hate Bayern.

With the exception of a few rare moments like this, playing at the Allianz Arena became a burden. Every *Sechzig* fan that I spoke with wants to return to the club's traditional home at Grünwalder Stadion in Giesing, a working-class region of Munich. During several games at the Allianz Arena, the 1860 Munich ultras will display a banner reading, *Alle wege führen nach Giesing* (All the roads lead to Giesing). 'Of course I would love to play in the Grünwalder, but that is not realistic in the near future sadly,' Giko says. 'There are too many awful contracts that would need to be broken and I don't see us spending as much money as we would need to do that. I don't see that happening, as long as we don't get relegated.'

The club played at Grünwalder for eight decades, from 1911 to 1995, ironically with Bayern as their tenants between 1925 and 1972, before both clubs moved to Munich's Olympic Stadium (a legacy of the 1972 Summer Olympics) and finally to the Allianz Arena from 2006 onwards (although TSV 1860 moved back to the old ground several times, especially between 1982 and 1995). However, it was at Grünwalder, a gift box-shaped stadium, that 1860 Munich experienced their golden era, winning a German Cup in 1964 and the club's first and only Bundesliga title in 1965/66.

At the time of my visit, the stadium was currently being used as a training facility and as 1860 Munich's reserve team stadium. The Grünwalder is currently owned by the city, although it is colloquially known in the region as *Sechz'ger* (*Sechzig*'s stadium). Its current capacity is for 12,000 people, dramatically smaller after being destroyed during World War II. The stadium is a symbol of an era when 1860 was the greatest team in Munich.

Yeah, you read that correctly. TSV 1860 Munich was once the greatest team in the city of Munich. At least, more precisely, the first team in Munich to win the Bundesliga and also a founding member of the German national league in 1963. Unlike the dynamic involving Espanyol and Barça, for example, where the popular team has always been the biggest throughout history, *Sechzig* fans subconsciously feel like they support a big club.

Before the 1960s and the foundation of the Bundesliga, German football was divided into regional tournaments where the winners would play for the national title in knockout style. When the German Association came up with the idea of a league, the inaugural season had only room for one team per city. 1860 Munich played the first Bundesliga as the Bavarian champions.

They won the Bundesliga in 1966, and finished second a season later, losing by only two points (Bayern finished seventh). During five consecutive years, the Lions experienced times of glory, which ultimately proved to be their only five years of glory. They somehow awakened a giant in the city, something that I have personally dubbed the 1860 Theory of Karma. Let me explain:

- In 1964, they won the DFB German Cup. Bayern Munich won the same tournament in 1966, 1967 and 1969 (not mentioning other decades).

- In 1965, they reached the UEFA Cup Winners' Cup Final (and lost to West Ham). Bayern Munich not only won the same tournament in 1967, but the most prestigious European Cup a decade later (in 1974, 1975 and 1976).[2]

---

2   The tournament that today is known as the UEFA Champions League.

- In 1966, they won their only Bundesliga. Bayern Munich won the same league for the first time in 1969. And 28 more times after that.

It has always been like a Bayern thunderstorm in response to some 1860 Munich drizzle. My theory may expand to even before the foundation of the Bundesliga, when football was definitely not the biggest concern in Germany. 1860 Munich finished second in the German national championship in 1931. Bayern Munich won the same title a year later in 1932, which was their only trophy before they became the European powerhouse we now know today.

The discrepancy between the two clubs never stopped growing. And after so many years in Bayern Munich's shadow, the average age of an 1860 Munich supporter went up. 'It is obviously really hard to win new supporters, the lower the level your team plays, and it has been over a decade since 1860 played in the Bundesliga for the last time,' says Giko. 'Our supporters are loyal and for the most part we have a good sense of humour. We even joke about our failures. Maybe you could throw in dreamy as well, because it's as close to a running gag as it gets that 1860 is going to be promoted next year, and next year and next year ... Sure, lots of young fans get raised to be a Lion by their parents who were part of the more successful years.'

It is hard to establish the exact point when the club became a shadow of Bayern. Theory of Karma aside, the *Sechzig* had several bad administrations on top of the other, decades of financial mistakes and bad decisions. Only four years after winning the Bundesliga, for instance, the club was relegated to the second division for the first time. In the 1980s, the team played in the fourth division after not paying the German Revenue Agency. And in the 1990s the club went into another financial crisis after hiring questionable stars in the final stages of their careers, such as Abedi Pelé and Davor Suker. Finally, in 2004, the club plunged into debt by taking over the consortium of the Allianz Arena. But, hey, if you'd rather not talk about the x's and o's, there are definitely two moments in the club's past that *changed history forever.*

Take a ride in the DeLorean and travel back in time to Franz Beckenbauer's childhood, when he was growing up in the Giesing area as a *Sechzig* supporter. According to Uli Hesse,[3] Beckenbauer had a dream to play for 1860 Munich, like his idol Kurt Mondschein. It was during an under-14 city tournament in 1958 that he changed his mind, as he played for his local team SC Munich in the championship final. After he complained about a tackle, Beckenbauer was slapped in the face by an 1860 player. So, he joined Bayern Munich instead.

Now travel in time to a few years later, to Gerd Müller's city of Nördlingen. The phenomenal goalscorer had been scouted by several clubs in Bavaria and it was 1860 Munich that came up with the best deal. However, the club's manager missed his train and was not able to meet up with the future star, who ended up signing with Bayern instead. But not only that, as the story goes, Müller allegedly thought during the whole meeting that he was in fact signing to play for 1860!

---

3   Hesse, U., *Bayern: Creating a Global Superclub* (London: Yellow Jersey, 2016)

The club missed an opportunity to sign two German football legends. And right after that, in 1973, when Eintracht Braunschweig put a Jägermeister logo on their shirts without asking permission, the DFB decided to authorise jersey sponsorship in German football. Bayern Munich immediately signed a lucrative contract with Adidas, starting from April 1974. At the time, 1860 Munich was playing in the second division, so all the club could come up with as their main sponsor was Frucade, a local soft drink.

However, regardless of what really happened, bad administration or bad luck, missing trains or not, 1860 Munich supporters chose to blame Bayern for their club's collapse. 'We need to beat Bayern again and hopefully that will happen in the coming years,' Luis Lessner says. 'I think Munich needs both of their clubs in the first division, for historical reasons and to make the rivalry more interesting. It has always been red, against the blues.'

Not much is needed to make an 1860 supporter say negative things about Bayern. 'There is no opponent, imaginary or real, that I wouldn't root for in a game against Bayern,' Giko says. 'They destroy upcoming teams and belittle the Bundesliga. They made me lose most of my interest in the Bundesliga because they have turned the entire league into farm teams. I hate their guts! I can't stand the players and their average arrogant supporter and everything they stand for.' He also claimed, of course, that Bayern Munich is helped by the referees.

The majority of the 1860 Munich ultra chants behind the goal are against Bayern. There are countless variations of *Scheiß FC Bayern* (Bayern is shit), sometimes to a

'Guantanamera' melody or simply shouted by the ultras and repeated by the whole stadium. The atmosphere at the stadium was great, even with a semi-empty crowd (24,000 is a lot of people, but not ideal for a place with a capacity of 75,000). Before the kick-off, there were pyrotechnics and a mascot running around. The fans sang 'You'll Never Walk Alone', a song adopted by 11 other clubs from Germany. In case an alien arrived on Earth on that cold evening, it would've never imagined that the game was a battle against relegation to the third division.

Some might say that losing something is worse than never having it at all. Munich is a very rich city and 1860 fans feel like they should have a bigger share of the football pie. It is easy to find a Bayern souvenir in every touristy part of the city. As for the 1860 merchandising, I could only find it in a small shop near Viktualienmarkt square. The rivalry has cooled over the years, with the dynamic being that 1860 Munich cares a lot about Bayern, but not the other way around. It has been more than a decade since they played against each other.

In all fairness, I also spoke with a couple of FC Nürnberg fans, a club that won the German championship nine times, with a fanatic fan base, and they don't consider playing against 1860 Munich a Bavarian derby either. They immediately refused to be associated with a 'small club'. Their Bavarian derby is only against the big boys of Bayern Munich.

The Munich derby, sometimes, is even less important to Bayern Munich players. During a German Cup quarter-final match in 2008, for instance, 1860 Munich forced extra time, before Miroslav Klose was famously knocked down one metre *away from the box* (Franck Ribéry scored a cheeky penalty that sent Bayern through). The players barely celebrated as they walked off the pitch. We cannot say the same when 1860 Munich won the derby for the last time in April 2000. After defeating Bayern's Oliver Kahn, the 1860 players threw themselves on the ground, some of them crying and being carried off the field by their fans. Since the Bundesliga was introduced in 1963, 1860 Munich have won the derby only nine times in 38 meetings.

Nearly all these victories fit in with the 1860 Theory of Karma. As it follows:

- In 1969, they won 2-0. Bayern Munich won their first Bundesliga ever.
- In 1970, they won 2-1. 1860 Munich finished the season relegated.
- In 1977, they won 3-1. 1860 Munich finished the season relegated again.
- In 2000, they won twice, 2-1 and 1-0. Bayern won the Bundesliga.

In the latter, Bayern Munich won the league on the last day, on goal difference. However, as mentioned earlier, 1860 Munich at least qualified for the UEFA Champions League in 2000/01, which gave origin to a book called *The Incredible Success of 1860 Munich* (translated from German). But not quite so, really. The team was eliminated in the qualifying round (by Leeds United) and Bayern were the champions (on penalty kicks!).

Currently 1860 Munich has 18,600 members while Bayern has 277,000, the football club with the largest membership in the world. With such a gap in resources, and not facing each other on a regular basis, *Sechzig* lowered their expectations when they came face to face with Bayern. Fans will turn up to see the amateur derbies (an alternative team with under-19 players). 'It is the closest Munich gets to a real derby right now so the atmosphere is amazing,' Giko says. 'The game is sold out every time. Many of the 1860 ultras boycott the Allianz Arena and watch the games of our *Amas* [amateurs] instead because they play in the Grünwalder. It's the highlight of our season and that's what you get to see and hear during the derby.'

It may seem a little depressing to face an alternative version of a local rival, but sometimes fans fall in love with a football team for the strangest reasons. 'My first away game was against Wacker in Burghausen [110km west of Munich],' Giko says. 'It was at night and sometime during the match, the lights went off and everything went dark. That was over ten years ago, so my memories are kind of blurred, but it's still there. My dad took me to this game.'

Luis Lessner and Giko never saw their team play in the first division. And yet, Luis, a 6ft 2in-tall man with blue eyes and blond hair tied in a samurai style, is an unconventional optimist. 'Sometimes it is good to be the worst, I really think, because then you can only go up,' he says, in a true German way, with no hint of irony. 'Especially for younger fans, we can build on our character as fans. It is important to remain loyal to our team, even if we won't always win.'

After one more desperate attempt to again be relevant, in 2011 the club sold 60 per cent of its shares to a 34-year-old Jordanian businessman billionaire, Hasan Ismaik. He became the owner of the club, but he could not technically control the football department, where he is only entitled to 49 per cent of the votes because of Germany's 50 per cent plus one rule (ensuring clubs hold the majority of their own voting rights to protect them from the influence of external investors).

Ismaik proved himself to be a delusional type, stating that in ten years the club would be 'at the Barcelona level'. He proposed to build a new stadium on the old Munich airport site, which is next to a zoo, so all the lions would be named after an 1860 Munich player (the city council rejected the idea). He then came up with the plan of rebuilding the Grünwalder Stadion (without the zoo and lions!) with a capacity for 36,000 people, also rejected by the city.

Even if he's not a billionaire football investor, it seems like Lessner has a more realistic plan. 'What we really need is stability, a four- to five-year plan without changing the head coach every year,' he says. 'Every bad season makes everyone desperate. We fired six head coaches in the last two years. It can't be like that!' Brazilian football fans are very accustomed to this model of firing coaches, I told Lessner. He said that was probably the reason Germany beat Brazil 7-1 in the 2014 World Cup semi-final. To which I asked him how it felt to support so many Bayern Munich footballers playing for the national team. We both laughed, nervously.

On that glorious night of second division football, 1860 Munich easily beat FC Nürnberg 2-0, with both goals in the first half. 'Glad you picked one of the few times we won,' Giko says. 'Otherwise you'd have to watch the horrendous display of football I'm forced to see week in and week out.' What a magnificently German way to celebrate a massive victory!

It is understandable, though, as the club has been facing relegation for several years, only to escape at the last minute every time. In 2016, 1860 Munich escaped in their final match. 'We needed to win to not go down to the third division, and we gave away a goal in the first minute,' Giko says. 'It took us 78 minutes to even up the score, my voice was long gone, but everybody was screaming like their life depended on it. The atmosphere basically exploded when we made it 2-1 in injury time. I hugged random people for minutes, not being able to process what we actually did.' Alright, *that* is the German way to celebrate.

I really like these personal accounts because they are relatable. Everyone reading this probably has a similar story about a last-minute goal celebration, no matter if you support Manchester United or Macclesfield Town. It is a singular passion, sometimes idiotic even, that makes every football fan understand each other. And I especially like that particular account because I know what happened next to 1860. And if you paid close attention, you know too.

Three months later and eight consecutive defeats after beating FC Nürnberg, there was no happy ending this time. In front of 62,200 fans at the Allianz Arena, 1860 Munich lost 2-0 to Jahn Regensburg and was relegated to the third division. The game was interrupted for 15 minutes with the fans throwing seats on the pitch (they are all Bayern's seats, after all). The billionaire owner, Hasan Ismaik, refused to pay the licence to play in 3. Liga, alleging a plot against him by the club's directors, and 1860 Munich was relegated to the fourth division instead. The irony of it all is that the club could finally return to play at its beloved Grünwalder Stadion.

Above all possible explanations on how the club became so small compared with their giant neighbours, the simplest is that 1860 Munich was too good too soon. When football became increasingly professional in the 1970s, with sponsors and TV rights, Bayern Munich was successful at the right time. How far can a fan base resist based solely on their past? How much damage can a football investor make? 1860 Munich was the first club from the city to win the Bundesliga and that will never change. But what happens to them now?

A few weeks after that game, I had to return to Munich to catch a bus to Turin at Fröttmaning, which is across the viaduct from the Allianz Arena. The stadium is the first thing you see from the road, as I saw an incredible red and white horde of people coming out of the subway. In three hours Bayern was about to play at home, and last-minute tickets for Bayern's games are practically impossible to get (I naively checked it out). Instead I took that opportunity to share some *biers* with Bayern's fans at the bus station pub. I asked them how they feel about their local rivals. Although with somewhat different responses, they all kind of said the same thing: 'Nobody supports 1860 in Munich.' Well, I had just seen 24,000 of them who do.

Next stop: Berlin, Germany
Distance: 585km (364 miles)
How to get there: Six hours by bus
The best advice: Beer is cheaper than water and you can drink alcohol in public spaces
Soundtrack: 'Autobahn' by Kraftwerk

CHAPTER 4

BLOOD FOR UNION BERLIN

Union Berlin 2-0 TSV 1860 Munich
Stadion An der Alten Försterei
Friday, 24 February 2017
2. Bundesliga (Second Division)
Attendance: 20,176

It is an anthropological experience watching a game at Stadion An der Alten Försterei, roughly translated to 'Stadium at the old forester's house'. As soon as you step outside the Köpenick station, it is like you've entered a time capsule into East Berlin, surrounded by unpainted brick housing blocks and other signs of communist architecture. From the station, a walk to the stadium is through a forest (and there is an old forester's house there). Opened in 1920, the *An der Alten Försterei* has that old-fashioned appearance, terraced on three sides and seats only in its tribune stand – around 3,500 seats for a total capacity of 22,000.

At least where I was supposed to sit down, at the north zone (*ecke nord*), adjacent to where the ultras stand behind the goal, it made no difference anyway. Everybody was standing for the whole game, practically in front of the traditional manual scoreboard, a brick wall with a small window for staff to swap the score numbers. The terraces were covered, but the roof was so low that it made the noise reverberate even louder. It was like being in 1987, but without the Wall.

The Clash, The Buzzcocks and The Undertones blasted on the speakers before kick-off.

Players came onto the pitch to the sound of the club's official anthem, Nina Hagen's 'Eisern Union' (she was from East Berlin and her father was a diehard Union supporter). Everyone raised their club's red and yellow scarves up in the air, and sang the song, which goes like this: 'We from the East always go forward, shoulder to shoulder for the Iron Union.' The club's nickname *Eisern Union* (Iron Union) is a clear reference to its working-class roots. When the song stopped, Union's ultras at *Waldseite* (the forest stand) started screaming *Eisern*, so the crowd at *Gegengerade* (the opposite stand) responded with *Union*, and back and forth it went, louder and louder, until the chanting broke into applause. There's probably a German word for it.

The stadium's atmosphere is unique, even peculiar if you will. When Union's players are announced on the big screen before kick-off, the fans scream *Fußballgott* (Football's God), and when the opponent players are called out, they scream *Na Und!* (So what?). Football chants tend to be pretty much all the same everywhere in Germany, although Union Berlin's ultras are not fooling around when it comes to winning the Grammy for Best Football Chants. The lyrics of *Unsere Liebe. Unsere Manschaft. Unser Stolz. Unser Verein* (Our love. Our team. Our pride. Our team.) got stuck in my head for days, and are spread all over the stadium. They also have a cool rendition of Monty Python's 'Always Look on the Bright Side of Life'.

What really caught my attention, though, and it felt almost like a battle song, was the chant *Dem Morgenrot Entgegen* (Towards the Dawn), a song originally written in 1907 as a march anthem for the Labour movement (adapted to Union Berlin lyrics). Its melody resembles a pre-war chorus, with all the fans spinning their scarves above their heads. It is catchy and repetitive, but too complicated for me to repeat with the four German words I know.

Not only anthropological, a game at An der Alten Försterei is unforgettable, as authentic as a football-watching experience possibly could be. It's different from elsewhere: it doesn't have St. Pauli's cult status, or the tension at Millwall's Den, or the religious experience of Torino. It is primal and naive all at once, as if the match was not even related to a league table, but instead, a cathartic experience in itself. It may even sound a bit nostalgic, but it is how the Union Berlin supporters feel like it should be; they sweat and bleed for their club. As for me, again, I felt like I was transported back to the 1980s when I started watching, playing and loving football. A period of time that was far from easy if you lived in East Berlin.

Frank Bierkholz, 52, and Lutz Redlich, 53, are cousins and with them they bring Juliane, 31, who sort of acted like their spokesperson. The generational difference is obvious for many fans, especially because they have different memories. 'The [Berlin] Wall was never present in my life, so it is different for me than how it used to be for Frank and Lutz, who are very reserved,' Juliane says. 'The younger fans don't know or don't care about Union's past, as it doesn't make sense to them. They just want to have fun, drink and chant at the stadium.'

The cousins started supporting the Union because it was the available option in their region. Frank was born in Neuruppin, a town 90km north-west of Berlin in former East Germany, and now works as a sailing instructor. Lutz works for a crane manufacturing company and went to his first game in 1978. He was born in Hennigsdorf, a district that shared its border with West Berlin, so he grew up less than 2km from the Berlin Wall. His only access to East Berlin was through a canal checkpoint built as a bypass to avoid passage through to the West.

Berlin has never been a football powerhouse in Germany (either before or after reunification). Union Berlin's neighbouring team from the West, Hertha Berlin, was never remotely giant. The rivalry had always been prevented by the Wall separating them. However, Union Berlin's history included a bigger giant to battle against, something larger than a football club: the Stasi team, the official State Security Service of East Germany. It sounds a little melodramatic, I reckon, although in practice that was exactly what the country's football teams had to fight against before the Berlin Wall fell in 1989 (and, of course, not only football teams battled them). Here's a little context before we can move forward.

When the socialist regime took power in East Germany after World War II, a barrier with the West was put in place (metaphorically and physically when the Wall was built in 1961). It had become impossible for football teams to hire players from the other side of the Wall. Eastern teams had to develop players by themselves in a reduced population.

The big clubs from East Germany at the time, Dynamo Dresden and Dynamo Berlin, struggled in the European tournaments. Not only that, but from 1974 to 1983, the country saw a West German team reach the European Cup Final seven times (Bayern Munich won three; Hamburger once), many times eliminating a team from the poorer side of Germany in the process. FC Magdeburg was the only East German team to win an international competition when in 1974, they beat AC Milan in the European Cup Winners' Cup Final (they currently play in the third division).

The clubs struggled with the lack of exchange, but it was worse for the fans. In the 1970s and 80s, East Germans travelled to socialist countries like Yugoslavia and Czechoslovakia to see live West German football (a visa was not required for these visits). They couldn't see these games anywhere else, not even when the Western teams played in East Germany.

According to Alan McDougall, ticket allocation managed to keep out undesirable elements. 'Of the 19,000 tickets released for Dynamo Berlin's European Cup match against Austria Vienna in September 1985, 6,500 were sold to Stasi and Interior Ministry officials. A further 6,900 tickets were allocated to pre-selected outlets including customs and police officers. This left at the most 5,600 tickets, less than one-third of the capacity at the stadium for ordinary fans,' he writes.[4] That would be far worse if Dynamo's opponents came from England or West Germany.

---

4   McDougall, A., *The People's Game: Football, State and Society in East Germany* (Cambridge: Cambridge University, 2014)

The secret police of the GDR (German Democratic Republic) were linked to the Ministry for State Security, one of the largest spy operations in the world, to monitor its own population. It had 300,000 employees in a country of eight million, one secret agent for every 26 people. Before the Berlin Wall was built in 1961, more than 20 per cent of the country's population fled to West Germany, hence the 'necessity' for intense surveillance. According to Anna Funder in *Stasiland*, the Stasi 'knew who your visitors were, whom you telephoned, and it knew if your wife slept around. [...] Overt and covert, there was someone reporting to the Stasi on their fellows and friends in every school, every factory, every apartment, every pub ... for forty years.'[5]

Any individual accused of any wrongdoing would be in danger. Football players had no special treatment and could not leave. Dynamo Berlin's striker Lutz Eigendorf defected to West Germany to play for Kaiserslautern in 1979 and four years later suddenly died in a car accident at the age of 26, at the time reportedly driving under the influence of alcohol. He was actually murdered by the Stasi, as official documents indicated in 2000.

The foundation of Dynamo Berlin itself came as a direct order from General Erich Mielke, the head of the Stasi, who felt that the capital lacked a strong championship contender. In 1953, Mielke ordered the relocation to Berlin of all the players from Dynamo Dresden (the East German police's team), who won the national title that season, to form a brand-new Stasi team. General Mielke was not even into goals, dribbling and skills. 'Football success will

---

5   Funder, A., *Stasiland: Stories Behind the Berlin Wall* (London: Harper Perennial, 2003)

highlight more clearly the superiority of our socialist order in the area of sport,' he said. (General Franco, a prominent anti-communist figure, used football for the same type of propaganda during his long regime in Spain. It's not an ideological thing, it's a dictator thing.)

Meanwhile, in the 1960s East Berlin came up with another strong team, Vorwärts Berlin, the GDR's army team, that won six national leagues, before relocating to Frankfurt (Oder) on the East German–Polish border. Yes, that is right: the three most successful football clubs in East German history are the Stasi team, the army team and the police team.

Dynamo Dresden came back stronger in the 1970s, winning five national titles, so General Mielke used the same strategy as before: all Dresden players were transferred to their capital brother so that history could repeat itself. It worked quite well for Dynamo Berlin this time around: the club won ten consecutive leagues from 1979 to 1988. The team was allegedly favoured by the referees as well, and became known as 'The Eleven Pigs'. In the middle of this political turmoil was a small club with a working-class fan base called Union Berlin.

Fußballclub Union Berlin as we know today was founded in 1966, when every club from East Germany became a 'football club' entity separated from a 'sports club'. However, its origins can be traced back to 1906 from the industrial district of Oberschöneweide, home of the world's largest electrical company at the time (a gentrified neighbourhood today, like many areas in Berlin). It had essentially a blue-collar fan base, increasingly popular and with no affiliation to institutions. The club has always been a yo-yo type, before and after the Berlin Wall. They played 19 seasons in the GDR first division, but never even slightly came close to a title. The only glory for Union Berlin was an East German Cup in 1968, as huge underdogs.

The club was in the shadow of Dynamo, both in its football and politics. Union Berlin never beat their local rivals during their span of ten consecutive titles, including an 8-1 thrashing in 1986, a disaster for the goalkeeper Wolfgang Matthies, considered an all-time Union Berlin favourite. For security reasons, derbies were played on neutral ground, at Stadion der Weltjugend, since Dynamo's stadium in Prenzlauer Berg was steps away from where the Berlin Wall once stood (a 30-metre stretch still exists today and is used by graffiti artists).

However, Union Berlin supporters did not care as much about results and they would constantly challenge the authorities – their football rivals were ultimately Stasi members. There are conflicting reports indicating that Union fans used to shout *Die Mauer muss weg* (The Wall must fall) before Dynamo's free kicks (a play on words with the football wall). According to a feature published on the BBC,[6] the fans also chanted *Wir wollen keine Stasi schweine* (We don't want Stasi swine). In one particular game, benches were ripped out and the stadium trashed. However, there is a tendency to romanticise that history, as if it were a Rocky Balboa vs Ivan Drago fight.

Yes, it was an intense derby, and yes, Union Berlin fans continue to hate Dynamo's guts, whom up to this day, they still refer to as the 'government's team'. On the other hand,

---

6   Evans, S. (12 July 2014). The secret police with its own football team. BBC.

hooliganism started to spread all over Europe in the 1980s and East Germany was not immune. Especially amongst the GDR fan bases, when the country began to disintegrate, between 1985 and 1988. Young males were discontent with the country's economy, lack of opportunities, government isolation, and, well, life in general. It is worth noting that in their minds that way of living would last forever, since they had no idea what would happen in November 1989.

Many supporters at that time would attend games only as a subversive act. A group of the Union Berlin fan base was the subject of the documentary *Und freitags in die Grüne Hölle* (Fridays at the Green Hell), a reference to a local pub where they used to meet in Prenzlauer (which no longer exists). The film provides a unique picture of everyday life of youth in the GDR and of hooliganism. Supporters sing and drink dressed in 'subversive clothing', wearing long hair, mullets and moustaches (a lot of moustaches!), which was not recommended by the socialist regime (needless to say, the movie was banned and not properly released until 2006). It is a must-see for those interested in football, history and the GDR, and it's available online, with no English subtitles, on the website of the bpb (Federal Centre for Civic Education).

When it comes to the mystique about Union Berlin fans and their political defiance, the club's press spokesman, Chris Albeirt, is not openly affirmative: 'We do have a very unique history, compared to other clubs,' said Arbeirt to *Deutsche Welle* in 2011. 'But it wasn't us that always claimed we were this big anti-Stasi club. These are stories that get over-amplified in the media.'[7]

---

7   Knight, B; Isenson, N. (29 July 2011). Berlin's FC Union wrestles with its East German past. *Deutsche Welle*.

The anti-government proclamations are somewhat blurred in history, but Union's rivalry against Dynamo was very, very real. After the reunification, Union Berlin got their epic revenge when they beat the former Stasi club 8-0 for a third division game in front of 14,020 fans at An der Alten Försterei. Chaotic scenes taken from a crappy phone camera are available on YouTube, with the fans' redemption on full display. Without GDR's official support, Dynamo Berlin succumbed to lower divisions, currently in the fifth division. At the time of writing, the last derby was played in 2006. It is a dead rivalry for the post-Wall generation of fans.

So where does Hertha Berlin fit in this story? Well, West Berlin was an enclave entirely inside East Germany (its nearest West German town was 160km away, only accessible by checkpoints). Technically it was the same city, although in different countries, and it was not uncommon for East Berliners to support a club from the West. As for the Union fans, their neighbours in Hertha were a natural choice. In the documentary *Und freitags in die Grüne Hölle*, a Union fan appears wearing a denim jacket with a Hertha Berlin patch.

Think about it like this: Union and Hertha stadiums were separated by a distance no further than the distance separating Arsenal from Tottenham (Manhattan from Brooklyn, for the *soccer* fans). In daily life, however, they were on different planets, so to speak. The friendship between the fans became a fanzine, *Union und Hertha – eine Nation* (Union and Hertha: One Nation). Immediately after reunification, the two teams played a friendly match known as the Peace Game where more than 50,000 fans turned up at Berlin Olympiastadion.

The friendship from the past is non-existent these days, but also, there is no history for us to call the Berlin derby a rivalry. The first time they faced each other in an official game was only in 2010, in the second division. Hertha plays in a pompous stadium (in its size and its architecture), while the Union stadium used to be a forester's house. On the other hand, the ambience at Olympiastadion is cold and flat with a running track separating players from the crowd, while at Försterei, the players feel the fans breathe on their necks. Union Berlin fans are mostly middle-class workers from the East, while Hertha fans represent the multicultural Berlin.

Berlin has been an epicentre of alternative lifestyles since the 1970s, a favourite place to settle whether you are a punk, hippie or squatter – or now, a millennial hipster. Hertha's stadium has had a 64 per cent average occupancy rate in the last decade, lower than the Bundesliga average of 92 per cent (the club plans to leave for a smaller and more compact stadium by 2025), and I can only speculate why they are not a massively supported club, considering Berlin is one of the largest and richest cities in Europe. It seems like, perhaps, Berliners (and non-Berliners) don't have enough room in their lives to care about their local club. I attended a Hertha game against Eintracht Frankfurt and the crowd was not anywhere near as vocal as what I'd witnessed a night earlier at Union stadium, even though they were a much bigger crowd of 43,000. There is an undeniable aura about the Olympiastadion, a venue where 'Jesse Owens defied Nazism', but also an undeniable sense of entertainment in the air. I got a ticket by wandering around the front of the stadium where a teenager sold me one half-priced (he had a birthday party to go to). That would be unthinkable at Försterei where tickets are sold out weeks in advance.

When it comes to rivalry, West Berlin never had another traditional football club. The blue and whites are a historical club, with two national titles won in the 1930s, megastores in shopping malls and big billboards around the city; they are perceived as a rich club. That is why they recently spent way too much money on countless Brazilian flops (the exception being Marcelinho, a fan favourite who spent six years at the club; so in case you don't remember him, that pretty much says it all about his football status). All this digression serves only to say that Union and Hertha became strangers playing in the same city, as opposed to their brotherhood from the past, while they were in different countries.

Three decades after the Wall went down, it is safe to say that Union fans no longer have a political identity or a legacy of hooliganism. On the contrary, the stadium is a friendly environment. 'The commercial aspect is not important to us; the fans and the atmosphere is what counts most and you don't feel like a customer but a family; that's why we love our team,' Juliane says.

Lutz is clearly the most diehard fan of the trio who took me to the stadium, knowing stats, and the x's and o's of the game (he even watched on TV the 1860 Munich game I attended earlier that week). He never stopped following the club, not even when he lived in Stuttgart for work. He was only 12 when he attended his first game, with all the complications of travelling in East Germany, authorised by his mother. He witnessed everything possible related to

Union on the field, and he has a genuine passion for football. He doesn't like big screens or marketing campaigns. He doesn't even care about titles. 'Football to me is all this,' he says, in broken English, pointing to the fans drinking and laughing. I understood 100 per cent what he was saying.

Before kick-off, the stadium's surroundings are like a true *biergarten*. Lutz introduced me to a man selling merchandise from the trunk of a Trabant, the massively manufactured car in the GDR – aka The Worst Car Ever Built. He presented me with an ultras scarf (he told me to choose, but picked one himself after disagreeing with my choice). He paid for one, two, three, four beers, all coming with a collectible glass – well, there's some modern football to please fans, after all! It is safe to say that the German hospitality is absolutely something else.

After accessing the main gates, the stadium has a patio full of stalls of *currywurst* and beer vendors, the Union store, and toilets which are literally shipping containers. There were no toilets in the stands, as you need to use the one off the patio. The atmosphere is similar to an amateur Saturday morning game. The matchday programmes are sold in a Barkas minivan decorated in the colours of Union Berlin (the socialist version of Volkswagen's Kombi, a minivan used as a police car in East Germany). As a foreigner, it is sometimes easy to only associate the GDR with state surveillance, lack of diversity and repression, but a lot of people in the east part of Berlin still feel connected and proud about their East German origins.

During the game, Union supporters behave like, well, any football fan. They go mental at refereeing mistakes, calling them names, and they whine about bad plays. Lutz was on top of his game and he knew exactly who was the opponent's biggest weapon. He is not concerned about the possibility of Union being promoted to the Bundesliga for the first time in history. He doesn't want his team losing its identity. 'This is a good division and we don't need anything else,' he says. 'They [the German Federation] make a lot of demands to play in the Bundesliga and I would rather have the stadium as it is now, with no more seating. They change the schedule because of TV rights. We really don't need to change the character of our team.'

Union fans have been through a lot and they feel comfortable with where they are at. The club almost faced bankruptcy and played fourth division football as recently as 2006. They have been playing in the second division for nine years, never close to being relegated. Union supporters want to avoid a cult status, a 'hipsterisation' of the club like what happened to St. Pauli. The fans want Union to win their games of course, although they would rather not be promoted, and I had to argue that when a team wins a lot of games, it becomes inevitable that they wil gain promotion – or, can you imagine? – be the champions. They disavowed my prediction, as though I was speaking nonsense. It feels like playing in the most important division of Germany is something they never really thought about before.

Don't get me wrong, though: these fans are hardcore fans, capable of really intimate acts regarding their passion for Union Berlin. I will wrap this up with three stories:

1. After new safety rules were established to play in the second division, the stadium needed seats, a car park, a roof covering and an undersoil heating

system. The contractor abandoned the project in the middle, so the fans took up the job themselves. 2,400 volunteers showed up to rebuild the Stadion Försterei, offering up 140,000 hours of free labour. There is a monument honouring those who volunteered, made out of rusty metal, dressed in a Union Berlin safety helmet with a screwdriver and wheelbarrow. Lutz proudly showed me his name on the plaque. The fans only asked the club to keep the stadium's terraces.

2. In 2004, the fans organised a campaign, *Bluten für Union* (Bleed for Union), where they gave the money they received for donating their blood back to the club to keep it alive, all because Union needed €1.5 million for a licence to compete. Of course, it was a symbolic gesture, which was then followed by a regular ticket holder becoming the club's president (Dirk Zingler, owner of a logistics business for building materials). He is not a journeyman and the fans see him as someone who preserves Union's identity. He came up with the idea to play a friendly match against St. Pauli to raise more money since the two clubs share the same values of being against modern football and are *blutsbrüder* (blood brothers).

3. Union Berlin fans have been meeting up at Stadion An der Alten Försterei on Christmas Eve since 2013, to sing Christmas carols (and Union chants) for 90 minutes. It is seen as a farewell gesture before wrapping up for the German football winter break. In the first year, only 89 people showed up; however, since then the tradition has grown to almost 20,000 people annually. However, just like the Bundesliga promotion, Juliane is also not a big fan of the Christmas hype. 'It is not the same with so many people and many are not even from Berlin,' she says. 'I was there last year, but I'm thinking of not going this year.'

The club's identity is an obsession for Union supporters like Juliane, Lutz and Frank. They're radically against the Bundesliga, because as she would explain, other teams experienced a terrible fall after going up, such as her own father's football team Hansa Rostock (currently in the third division). The Berlin Wall went down nearly 30 years ago, although people from the east side are very suspicious. The Bundesliga is only a money sucker for them, as the licence to play costs more, the stadium needs a mandatory 8,000 seats, plus the obvious necessity to sign better players. Nine teams promoted in the past ten seasons went down the subsequent year (and a pair of those teams were then relegated to the third division).

It is a sensitive topic in Germany when one mentions the two former nations, as if only one became an over-achiever. The country deals with a visible economic gap between the East and the West up to this day. East German teams have struggled to play at the highest level. If during the communism era the clubs suffered from the lack of freedom to hire players, during the capitalist era, they have been suffering from the lack of money, quite simply. The region has no large companies and the population has dropped significantly. Only four clubs from the East played in the Bundesliga after reunification: Dynamo Dresden, Hansa Rostock (both now in the third division), VfB Leipzig and Energie Cottbus (in the fourth). RB Leipzig, a Red Bull-funded club with no connection to East Germany, is the only eastern team currently playing in the Bundesliga, as of the 2018/19 season. From the German national team that won the 2014 World Cup, Toni Kroos was the only player born on the east side.

Quite a coincidence, then, that his younger and not so talented brother, Felix Kroos, was the body and soul of Union Berlin on the pitch. He's been part of the club for four years, and like many other players, he is part of a long-term project. The most expensive player in the squad cost less than €1 million, not even half of what Mesut Özil receives every year from his Adidas sponsorship contract. At the end of every match, the crowd will not leave the stadium before greeting their players, whether they have lost or won.

A lot of Union favourites are players who spent years in the third or fourth division. I asked Lutz about the best player who ever played for the club, and he asked me back, with a lot of enthusiasm: 'Do you know Teixeira? He's one of our greats!' I did not, as I had to admit with total embarrassment (if I had €10,000 to spare, I would bet that you don't, either). Daniel Teixeira was a modest striker in Brazilian football, before moving to even more modest clubs in Germany. He became Union's top scorer in the third division in 2001 and returned to the club in 2006, leading the team to a promotion. Upon his retirement, Teixeira became the only Union Berlin player to ever receive a farewell match. I had to look him up to find out what he looked like.

The most valuable asset to a football club is the supporters. We used to hear that a lot, even knowing that these days we are just numbers on a spreadsheet. Nevertheless, Union Berlin wants to take that approach seriously. 'It is a football team that values the fans more than any other team because we actually have the right to say what happens to the team,' Juliane says. Administrative decisions are actually subject to popular consultation. 'It is a special atmosphere, as you can see for yourself. No matter how the team performs. It is also probably special because of the team's history connected to the history of East Germany.'

In 2011, the club sold the Alten Försterei stadium to the fans, in the form of 10,000 shares of €500 each, where each fan was able to acquire a maximum of ten shares. The idea behind this was to preserve the stadium's naming rights, so that it wouldn't be named after an automobile or insurance company brand. Are we surprised? The fans gave their blood to save the club, after all. 'We're selling our soul ... to the fans!' the president Zingler announced at the time. A football club that (sort of) fought against the socialist regime in the past has become a vocal leader against the capitalist concept of modern football. What a fascinating irony.

This is how a Union Berlin fan can see a football match for only €12.50 on a Friday night in one of the busiest nightlives in Europe, which is a real bargain. Union Berlin easily beat 1860 Munich 2-0 and after the game, snowflakes started falling on our heads while we all celebrated together (like a final scene from a cliché movie based on real events). Should I hope for the team to win the Bundesliga promotion, I asked? 'Let's hope we will win the last games in the league and maybe have a chance to play in a different league next year,' Juliane says, casually, not really convinced that it's a good idea. A couple of months later, Union finished in fourth place, their best performance in history. Not enough for promotion, though.

On my way back to my hostel, the trio left me at Potsdamer Platz, where less than 30 years ago there was a very famous wall, right down the middle. It used to be an abandoned location; however, today it has been transformed into a vibrant square with shopping malls, neon lights and futuristic buildings. It is a place that in some way symbolises two different cities. It is the same city as Köpenick where Union Berlin plays, although it definitely looks like another.

Next stop: Hamburg, Germany
Distance: 289km (180 miles)
How to get there: Three hours by bus
The best tip: FlixBus goes to every deep recess of Europe and it's cheap, so I don't mind doing free advertising for them
Soundtrack: 'Was ist ist' by Einstürzende Neubauten

CHAPTER 5

SOMETIMES ST. PAULI; ALWAYS ANTI-FASCIST

St. Pauli 5-0 Karlsruher
Millerntor-Stadion
Monday, 27 February 2017
2. Bundesliga (Second Division)
Attendance: 29,073

The last home game that St. Pauli played in the Bundesliga had been an 8-1 loss to Bayern Munich in May 2011. The match was the biggest defeat in the club's history; however, 25,000 fans would not leave the Millerntor-Stadion until they could give a final salute to the players. With the team relegated to the second division, they chanted and clapped, a tradition that has been maintained for years, no matter the game's outcome. The 2010/11 season was quite intense for St. Pauli fans. They won against their local rivals Hamburger SV for the first time since 1977. Immediately after the victory, St. Pauli finished off that season on a streak of 11 straight losses, ultimately leading the team to relegation.

Their frustration reached its peak level during a home defeat to Schalke 04, when a fan threw a plastic cup full of beer, hitting the linesman in the neck and causing him to collapse on the field. The game was unfinished with two minutes left to play. It was a football scandal in Germany, the first time since 1976 that an event of that nature had happened in the Bundesliga – not the gratuitous waste of beer, but a game interrupted due to a fan's misconduct.

Contrary to widespread belief, St. Pauli fans are football fans, nonetheless. Yes, they are activists, they care about social causes and they have strong political views, but they are not immune from wanting an epic goal in injury time, a nasty challenge to take down an opponent, or the three points on the table. I wanted to emphasise this here. St. Pauli fans have a different culture, but they are first and foremost football fans.

I also want to make it clear that I have no intention to diminish St. Pauli's mythology. The club's cult status is undeniable, and that is the reason we all know about St. Pauli in the first place, and not Karlsruher, FSV Zwickau or any other German lower-division team. That being said, my primary focus of curiosity about St. Pauli is what their fans think about the game itself (the results on the pitch). The football element is important to me because when we choose a team to support (normally as children), we couldn't care less about ideological beliefs.

I'm not writing a manual on 'How to Become a Football Fan', although the connection with a football team is normally made over something related to the beautiful game: the atmosphere at the stadium, a favourite player, or an epic goal scored in injury time (I will use this analogy as many times as possible). However, I was not in

Hamburg to force my beliefs and sentiments on to others, so if the St. Pauli fans are more interested in ideology, that is fine too.

Before the kick-off, I met the Scarecrows Sankt Pauli, an organised group of 15 members (St. Pauli have more than 400 official fan clubs registered). Georg Josuttis, 51, is not a stereotypical St. Pauli fan that people came to associate with the club. He has a university degree in philosophy and is training to be a psychotherapist (meaning, he is your regular, average fella). 'Everyone in the stadium wants us to win, but we don't want to sell our souls to do it, and perhaps this is our biggest difference compared to other fan bases: winning is not the most important,' Georg says. 'The brotherhood is what matters the most for us, and we can spend hours talking about questionable referee decisions. It happens that sometimes we switch to political issues.' Georg started following the team when he moved to Hamburg in 1984 to pursue his compulsory military service (Germany abolished conscription in 2011).

Otti, 41, on the other hand, is a stereotypical St. Pauli fan that people came to associate with the club. He's all tattooed, with a Mohawk hairstyle, a denim jacket full of patches, and spiked bracelets. He moved to Hamburg in 2010 from Bremen and he has followed St. Pauli ever since. 'I used to live on the streets, always on drugs, but now I am 40 and I couldn't live like that forever,' he says. 'I have my own tattoo shop now and I can provide for my son and my wife. I come to the stadium to meet up with friends. This is a club that accepts everyone.' Unlike Georg, though, Otti will not enter the stadium. He's more a meet and greet kind of a guy.

According to the Scarecrows' website, they were founded in 2013. 'Whether from the far north or the deepest south, we come from everywhere. Either fish heads[8] or skinheads[9] and creative minds of all ages. We are like ticks!'[10] Another member from the Scarecrows that I spoke to was Nick Oetje, a charismatic fella with a big smile, a long beard and tattoos, wearing a large reamer in his ear, thick-framed glasses and a Scarecrows St. Pauli scarf. He works as a carer in a facility for people with physical disabilities. Nick is one of only three people of colour I saw at the stadium. 'I've been attending games since 1993, and my favourite game was in 2011 when St. Pauli won 1-0 against our city rivals at their stadium,' he says. 'After that season, St. Pauli unfortunately got out of the Bundesliga, and our dream has always been to return [to the Bundesliga], so we can beat them [HSV] again at Millerntor.'

The victory over Hamburger SV in the derby in 2011 remains iconic amongst fans, and a photo of the St. Pauli goalkeeper Benedikt Pliquett kicking an HSV flag after the game has become legendary. He was born in Hamburg and started his career at HSV at 16, but never had a chance to play professionally until he crossed the city to rivals St. Pauli (he currently runs three sex shops in the St. Pauli neighbourhood). Rivalry is a fundamental part of football culture, and in fact 73.9 per cent of football fans claim they

---

8   *Fishkopp*, literally fish head, is a slur term for people from northern Germany.

9   The original subculture from the 1980s, associated with ska and reggae, not the neo-Nazis.

10 *Zecken*, literally translated as 'ticks', is a slur term to offend left-wingers, especially leftie punks.

would miss their rivals if they ceased to exist, according to Sky Sports Football Fans Census (2017). The Hamburg derby is probably the great unsung rivalry, since it is not always globally covered. Perhaps, the actual game of football is not indeed a priority to St. Pauli fans; however, it does become more important when they face Hamburger SV. Their rivalry is a huge deal.

There are 'I hate HSV' stickers everywhere around the St. Pauli neighbourhood (especially in the toilets of every underground pub). The greatest hit amongst the popular chants that I heard at Millerntor was *HSV ist scheiße, Sankt Pauli ist euer Super-Gau* (HSV is shit and St. Pauli is your worst nightmare). Pro tip: to fully appreciate German football culture, it is crucial to learn the word *scheiße* (shit). HSV is the most prestigious club in the city, and is an abbreviation for Hamburger Sport Verein (Hamburg Sport Club), except for St. Pauli supporters, for which it means *Hund Sport Verein* (Dog Sport Club). Hamburger SV fans, on the other hand, consider St. Pauli to be 'the city whores' because the club is situated in the city's red-light district and also because they consider them to be a 'sell-out club'.

The two teams don't play each other often, since St. Pauli only spent a total of eight seasons in the first division. There have been only 16 Hamburg derbies in the Bundesliga since 1963, and St. Pauli have won only twice. Perhaps the animosity increases exactly because derbies are few and far between, and that is why sometimes the energy leads to hate, and the hate leads to violence (the dividing line between violence and rivalry is a thin one). The political element has also increased this rivalry, especially in the last couple of decades.

The Hamburg city derby can be traced back to the post-war tournaments, when clubs from the same region faced each other several times a year. At the time, St. Pauli was the second major force in the northern region. 'I am fascinated with the history of the club after World War II, when St. Pauli played in the [knockout] finals of the national championship and made it to the semi-finals once [in 1948],' says Michael Pahl, 44, a journalist who runs a St. Pauli museum. 'Not many people know that we came close to winning a national championship. And never have come close since then,' he says. St. Pauli also won the Hamburg regional league in 1947 with their Wonder Eleven (*Die Wunderelf*), a team 'sponsored' by a butcher shop, where players were awarded sausages and meatballs in a time when food rations were normal.

In the late 1950s and into the early 1960s, St. Pauli returned to their anonymity. Michael Pahl has been a fan since 1987 and is the editor of the club's magazine. St. Pauli is more than 110 years old, but what everyone knows about the club is from the 1980s, when they had a massive transformation. When the *Totenkopf* symbol was brought to the stadium and became sort of an official club logo. 'I don't know if it's fair to say that St. Pauli has two different histories, but the fact is that the club got a completely new image, one that it continues to have today,' Pahl says. 'It made the club popular way beyond what would be reasonable, if you look at what the club has achieved in terms of titles and trophies, which is none,' he jokes.

It is also unfair to say that St. Pauli did not have a loyal fan base before the hype. In the 1977/78 season, for instance, during their first appearance in the Bundesliga, the average attendance came close to 15,000 per game, the maximum capacity of the Millerntor-Stadion at the time. Of course all this support went downhill through the early 1980s, with an average attendance of 3,000 per game, although it is worth noting that was a period when St. Pauli was relegated to the third division while their cross-city rivals Hamburger SV dominated Europe.

In the 1980s, in addition to winning the European Cup in 1983, Hamburger won three Bundesligas and one German Cup (they also reached the European Cup Final in 1980 when they lost to Nottingham Forest). Hamburger is astronomically bigger and richer, and the most popular football club in the northern region of Germany. Outside the enclave of the St. Pauli neighbourhood, the city of Hamburg is totally dominated by HSV fans. Because of the lack of derbies in the 1970s and 80s, the rivalry significantly cooled down. It became like a pinscher barking at a Dobermann. Many HSV purists consider Werder Bremen their true rival (the *Nordderby* has been held twice every season for 65 years, except in 1980/81).

However, if we talk about a tourism competition, St. Pauli wins big time. The Millerntor-Stadion has easy access and is surrounded by pubs, the red-light district and the port, while Hamburger's Volksparkstadion is far removed from the city centre. It is an odyssey to access, a 20-minute walk from the closest subway station, and right next to a cemetery (HSV fans can reserve a place for eternity there). Hamburger's stadium is big, modern, hosts big events, and represents everything that St. Pauli fans consider wrong about modern football: naming rights subject to sponsors and a soulless vibe, nothing like the intimate and pulsating atmosphere of the Millerntor. Their rivalry is a paradox because even St. Pauli's transformation into an 'alternative club' is thanks to Hamburger SV, to some extent.

When the hooligans took over Germany in the 1980s, HSV had been affected by neo-Nazi groups from the Action Front of National Socialists (based in Hamburg and since prohibited). French philosopher Eric Cantona once said that 'you can change your wife, and your religion, but never your football team', but many Hamburger fans did just that. They rejected nationalism, turned their backs on HSV and went to St. Pauli instead. It coincided with the *Hafenstraße* conflicts in 1981, when squatters of all kinds stormed empty public buildings in the neighbourhood, when the city and the police tried to evict them and all hell broke loose. St. Pauli residents became resistors and their club the headquarters for resistance. *Hafenstraße* has become a symbol of counterculture, and these days is a housing association, for refugees in particular. *Kein mensch ist illegal* (No one is illegal) is a St. Pauli mantra.

St. Pauli's goalkeeper Volker Ippig became an iconic figure, had been directly involved in the *Hafenstraße* conflicts, and had lived there himself for a while. He once put his career on hold to help set up a hospital in Nicaragua under the Sandinistas, before coming back to Hamburg and winning a Bundesliga promotion with St. Pauli in 1987 (priorities!). He played only for St. Pauli for his entire career and quit football prematurely at the age of 29, after breaking part of his spine during training. Volker currently works at the Hamburg docks (of course he does).

The *Hafenstraße* conflicts and the resistance to neo-Nazism were urgent causes that demanded action in the 1980s. The social engagement these days is more theoretical, with many people displaying flags and banners at Millerntor against racism, homophobia and capitalism. I saw a bit of everything in the stands: rainbow flags, Che Guevara flags, anti-G20 flags (Hamburg held the forum a couple of months later), anti-Trump flags and a Pro 15:30 banner, supporting a manifesto against TV scheduling (the Saturday 3.30pm TV slot used to be the time for football in Germany). At half-time, the ultras raised the banner *Con nazis no se juega* (We don't play with Nazis), in solidarity with Rayo Vallecano supporters.[11]

St. Pauli supporters became strongly engaged in the 1990s, when punk activist Sven Brux founded the fanzine Millerntor Roar in 1989, considered by many to be a foundational publication in Germany and plausibly one of the first Antifa football fanzines in the world. The manifestos published within heavily influenced club members, and St. Pauli officially banned any kind of racist chants or banners in 1991, the first club in Germany to do so. A theatre manager from the very popular street Reeperbahn, Corny Littmann, became the first openly gay man to serve as a football president from 2002 to 2010.

On the other hand, a club cannot control political ideology entirely. A week before my arrival in the city, St. Pauli was all over the news. First, when their kit supplier Under Armour, through its founder, stated that president Donald Trump was a 'real asset to the United States'. St. Pauli released a statement asking Kevin Plank

---

11   I believe you read that story in Chapter 2.

to reconsider his statement, 'in view of the company's many employees of migrant background, which also holds true for FC St. Pauli and its values'. A couple of days later, during a game against Dynamo Dresden, the infamous Ultras Sankt Pauli raised a banner that read, 'your grandparents burned for Dresden' (a reference to the 72nd anniversary of the Allied bombing in the city). The ultras justified their action by saying that far-right groups use the World War II tragedy as a form of German victimhood, a belief that was adopted especially by many East German ultras, such as Dresden's Ultras Dynamo. Despite their justification for the banner, St. Pauli officially apologised for causing offence.

It is precisely this potato salad kind of activism mixed with football that made St. Pauli globally known. The skull and crossbones became a brand, and as the story goes, the pirate flag was brought to the stadium in 1987 by punk rock veteran, Doc Mabuse, who, to be honest, I've seen in countless interviews telling the story, but every time in a different way (he was currently living in a trailer and allegedly supports Altona 93, an even smaller club from Hamburg). Mabuse does not believe in the St. Pauli hype, and he is not alone. Many supporters dislike the idea of an anarchist symbol having been appropriated by the club for the purpose of income. Surrounded by so much political ideology, St. Pauli has to constantly battle the necessity of money to run a football club. The Jolly Roger logo became the club's salvation, but also a curse.

In addition to two official St. Pauli stores, it is possible to find the club's merchandising everywhere in the area, regardless of if it is a skateboard shop, an H&M, or knock-off products on the streets. The more you walk around, the more it looks like a Lego set of skulls and crossbones. The St. Pauli Tourist Office, for instance, is not an information centre at all, but a souvenir store that also serves as a concert ticket retailer. The shop logo is the skull and crossbones, of course. The owner, Henning Bunte, wears a mandatory St. Pauli hoodie. 'St. Pauli is a very unique football club, and so is our neighbourhood, which without doubt is more visited now than it was before. Football has become almost as interesting as the strip clubs,' he jokes. 'But it is the people from here who will always continue supporting the team; it won't be the tourists.' These fans once saved the club from bankruptcy, when in 2003 they bought 140,000 T-shirts as part of the campaign *Retter* (Saviours), which were sold in McDonald's restaurants, of all places.

Henning is a friendly guy, and despite the misleading look of his store which could be off-putting to a passer-by, he is a very welcoming St. Pauli football fanatic. 'We recently played in the third division and I wouldn't like for us to play there anymore,' he says. 'The second division is alright; we're almost always playing there anyway.' What about playing in the Bundesliga again, I asked. 'It would be great, so we can drink and party for a while but it never lasts long. This is not a Champions [League] type of a football club, that's for sure,' he jokes.

St. Pauli is not a poor area in Hamburg and it has been gentrified in recent years. Rents have gone up and many art galleries, coffee shops and boutiques have opened up in the last couple of years. 'This has always been a region where everything changes,' Henning says. 'There were many sailors working at the port once or twice a week in the 1970s; that's why [to this day] we have a lot of bars and prostitution. The cargo containers killed tonnes of jobs and a lot of those people just left.' The population in the area dropped by 40 per cent between 1970 and 1985, and during the port crisis, workers became squatters and 'alternative types' started showing up at the stadium. There has been a visible change in the stadium, but also a political shift in the neighbourhood. In the 2017 national elections, the most liberal leftist party (*Die Linke*) finished as the fifth most popular party, with only 9.24 per cent of the votes. In the St. Pauli district alone, though, they received 33.8 per cent of the votes, which would be enough to finish first.

The region has been a bohemian destination since the 1960s. The Beatles played over 250 nights in Hamburg between 1960 and 1962 (Paul McCartney bought his iconic Höfner violin-shaped bass in the city). Reeperbahn Street is the neighbourhood epicentre, home to the largest number of sex shops, strip clubs and legal sex work in all of Europe. There is a McDonald's door to door to a strip club (and an official St. Pauli store). On Herbertstrasse the sex workers advertise their services from windows, but the street is safely protected behind a metal gate, a security measure to prevent the industry from becoming a tourist attraction (like it has become in the red-light district in Amsterdam).

St. Pauli, the region, is a 24-hour kind of place, covered in graffiti, and a self-deprecating humour floats about in the air. The people of Hamburg are proud to be local and they drink Astra, a beer with an unmistakable logo of an anchor and heart, sold for only €2 in bars. Hamburg is not as cool as Berlin or as clean as Munich. If Berlin is David Bowie, then Hamburg is The Clash – and Munich is definitely Coldplay. Hamburg is the most fun of all three cities.

It also became hard to avoid tourist traps, including the hostel I booked, with rooms all decorated with the St. Pauli logo (it was very cheap and a five-minute walk from the stadium, so give me a break here, alright?).[12] Its next-door building is the famous Jolly Roger bar, a 'supporter-owned' drinking hole, with hundreds of football stickers on the wall. It has a 1980s punk style and works as the fans' HQ before and after St. Pauli games. The place has an astonishing blasé atmosphere, a 'we're better than you' attitude that almost felt like I was in a TV sketch show (there are better bars down the same street). Its 'street cred' decoration is *most definitely* not enough if you want only to have a pre-match pint. It is too cool to be good.[13]

St. Pauli, the football club, has figured out a way to make money. They raise about €7.1m annually over merchandising sales – the fourth biggest seller in Germany, behind only Bayern Munich, Dortmund and Schalke 04. Their progressive identity is attractive to tourists and their stadium is very modern-*ish*. St. Pauli became a global brand, but is still a neighbourhood club. 'The club takes positions concerning political questions in the neighbourhood, supports local communities, and most fans still live in the neighbourhood,' says Michael Pahl. 'But of course, St. Pauli has many fans outside of Hamburg and even Germany.'

Grant, 26, an American living in Flensburg, 160km further to the north, contradicts the manual I was writing

---

12 Yes, I took it very personally and this is my one-star review.

13 Yes, it was not a great experience there too. I'm giving it two stars.

about 'How to Become a Football Fan'. He left the USA for a one-year exchange in a city near Hamburg and fell in love with the club (previously, he only liked *soccer* through FIFA video games). His first game in the stadium was in October 2008 against 1860 Munich. 'As it happened, it ended up being the season we got promoted back to the Bundesliga,' he says. 'St. Pauli won 2-0, I believe [yes, they did], so a drunk 1860 fan was mad at the result, and shouted "fucking foreigners" at us, and immediately St. Pauli fans around me intervened and told him to fuck off.'

I need to make this clear: it was the St. Pauli fans that, first and foremost, began acting as social activists (supporting refugees, protecting minorities, being Antifa, etc.). The club only naturally absorbed these ideas. St. Pauli is not politics linked to football; it is football linked to politics. 'I think the club and fan scene are important for the political mobilisation in Hamburg and I strongly agree with our fans' political positions,' Grant says. 'It's invaluable to both the club and to German soccer in general to be the voice against prejudice. Especially given how many clubs are so unwilling to do anything about Nazis in their stadiums.' Grant also understands the intricate matter of being a foreigner supporting a club seen as only fashionable by many. 'We do have a fair amount of "fans" who only care about being cool, or wear St. Pauli clothes,' he says. 'I know if we were to play in the fourth division, we would lose a lot of casual fans, but I don't find that is necessarily bad. People actually in the stadium are there because they love the club and want to see them win. I love St. Pauli no matter what league they play, even in the sixth division.'

The merchandising sales made St. Pauli somehow a brand, and the club's ethos has become as polarised as the Beatles vs Stones discussion. Depending on who you ask, the club is perceived as anti-capitalists, bad motherfuckers, or even sell-out corporates to others. On the other hand, the noisy roar and the incendiary atmosphere at Millerntor is ultimately what football is all about. The fans sing 'You'll Never Walk Alone' a cappella before kick-off, before the loudspeakers boom a punk rock version of *Das Herz Von St. Pauli* ('In the Heart of St. Pauli'), interrupted only by the iconic ringing bells of AC/DC's 'Hells Bells'. A frenzied stadium indicates that the two teams are coming on the pitch. The script has gone on for 15 years now, and it is probably always the same, but regardless, fantastic the first time one sees it. I was on the opposite side of the ultras (a ticket I purchased months in advance), with the ordinary people, families and seniors. Actually, there were more 'alternative types' outside than inside the stadium. The fans never stopped supporting, chanting and raising flags of all kinds, and they don't ever whistle at opponents – except at Hamburger's teams since *HSV ist scheiße* (shit).

The Millerntor is an all-seated renovated stadium for 29,500 fans. There are no terraces like at the Union Berlin stadium. Hot vendors sell five different types of sausages and Astra beer. The stands are very close to the pitch. During the warm-up, St. Pauli head coach Ewald Lienen, dressed in sports clothes, stood in front of the fans, bumping his chest and shouting 'St. Pauli! St. Pauli!'. When he was a footballer, Ewald once suffered a fractured, open femur while playing for Arminia Bielefeld, and he still managed to leave the field walking, definitely the kind of commitment that St. Pauli fans love and respect.

St. Pauli easily won 5-0 against Karlsruher on that freezing Monday night. Every goal celebration is muffled by Blur's 'Song 2' on the loudspeakers (I'm not a big fan of goal songs, which if we're being honest, is the definition of attending a modern football match). There is no song better than listening to thousands of people yelling when their team scores a goal. Turkish-born Cenk Şahin was the man of the match with four assists, three of them to German-Moroccan Aziz Bouhaddouz, a nice coincidence for a club with the motto of 'No one is illegal'.

At half-time, a supporter next to me said that I was lucky because neither the team nor the striker are nearly as good on a normal night. Christoph Sassenhagen is not a stereotypical St. Pauli fan that people came to associate with St. Pauli fans. His father used to play for Hamburger SV when he was growing up. 'I was raised in another part of the city where everyone supports "the other club" [HSV],' he says. 'My entire family also supported "the others" because of my dad, and they still do.' Chris is in his 50s and works for an infrastructure and logistics company. He moved to Stuttgart and when he came back to Hamburg in the late 1990s, he felt more connected with St. Pauli. 'I strongly believe in the club's policies because football is not an island kept apart from society,' he says. 'It is not acceptable that acts of racism are tolerated in stadiums, especially here in Germany. Football gives visibility to social causes and it makes it even more important to fight against injustices.'

Christoph cares about politics, but he's an avid football fan. He knows statistics, talks about goals and memories, and above all, he speaks enthusiastically about St. Pauli players from the past. The Sandinista goalkeeper Volker Ippig is mentioned, as well as Sonny Wenzel, St. Pauli's top goalscorer (88 goals). 'You need to check out Walter Frosch who once played with a pack of cigarettes in his socks!' he says. 'Froschi', as he was known, played six seasons for St. Pauli in the 1970s and died of cancer in 2013 at 62 – note the irony! – due to complications from smoking. A defender, he wore a Frank Zappa-style moustache, and was booked 27 times in 37 games during a season, leading the Bundesliga to adopt the one-game suspension for players after five yellow cards.

Great stories in small clubs are not usually related to winning great trophies. St. Pauli beat FIFA world champions Bayern Munich in 2002, a massive celebration of David overcoming Goliath, Christoph's favourite game at the stadium. The club's highest place in the first division was a modest tenth in the 1989/90 season; however, football fans experience joy and satisfaction with no regard for if their cause is trivial or not. 'There is a goal scored by Leo Manzi that prevented us from relegation to the third division once,' Christoph says. 'Ask anyone and they will remember the party after the game. Manzi had no technique, but a lot of heart.' What are the odds, but I knew exactly who he was talking about, since Leo Manzi played for my team, Internacional, in 1999. 'He was the only Brazilian who couldn't kick a ball,' Christoph jokes. We both laughed about it. Manzi scored only four goals for Inter. Chris was completely right.

Players who sweat and bleed for the club are widely recognised here. Fabian Boll, who played for the team from 2002 to 2014 (while working as a police officer), is the favourite player of many fans, including Grant, the American. 'We were down 0-2 against Dynamo Dresden once, and Boll came off the bench and completely took the game into his own hands, and we ended up winning 3-2 in the last few minutes.' The favourite game of Georg, from the Scarecrows, is the Fabian Boll farewell game. 'It was May 2014, the last home game of our long-time captain,' he says. 'The choreography after the game lasted over a quarter of an hour. It was incredible!'

The game that I attended against Karlsruher was sold out, and 29,000 people wouldn't go home until they saluted the players, chanting and clapping. It was Monday but the party had only started when I met the Scarecrows after the game. 'Third division never again!' Nick, from the Scarecrows, shouted. 'The results are not everything for us, but they make people happy.' He gave me a St. Pauli scarf. He passed me an Astra beer. St. Pauli spent a month undefeated and avoided relegation. They have been playing for nine straight years in the second division.

They might eventually go up one day, but how will they play competitive football in the first division without having lots of money? Then again, how do you make money without selling lots of fashionable hoodies (and becoming a brand)? In St. Pauli they need a casual fan base without the luxury of upsetting the real fans. I don't have the right answers, and it seems like St. Pauli fans don't either. Any of this wouldn't make any difference to a diehard fan at the end of the day. They will resist as they always have. With or without the skull and crossbones, there will always be epic goals scored in the last minute by unknown guys like Leo

Manzi that will keep the fans coming back. They have a different culture here, but they are football fans.

Next stop: London, England

Distance: 935km (580 miles)

How to get there: One hour 40 minutes by plane (according to Ryanair, it's a plane …)

The best advice: Don't tell the immigration officers anything about Millwall. Rather, say you're visiting somewhere quieter, like Buckingham Palace or the Emirates Stadium

Soundtrack: 'If the Kids Are United' by Sham 69

CHAPTER 6

FUCK OFF, I'M MILLWALL

Millwall 1-0 Peterborough
The Den
Tuesday, 28 February 2017
Football League One (Third Division)
Attendance: 8,032

In a dark tunnel under the railway on a blustery Tuesday evening, an hour after Millwall's horrendous football match, the visiting fans were unable to escape an ambush, probably orchestrated. They were attacked with bottles and bricks, and even though outnumbered, the lads shouted and threw punches back in the air. Everything was quick, tumultuous, frantic and chaotic. The entire brawl lasted no more than five minutes before the police appeared on the scene. The tunnel emptied and all the fans dispersed quietly in the direction of the train station.

It would have been terrifying, but NONE OF THIS *HAPPENED*.

The scene described above is just a passage from *Green Street*, a 2005 film about an American college student who moves to London and secretly becomes a hooligan (!), played by the Frodo Baggins actor (!) and directed by a German film-maker (!) for the North American audience (!). Everything per se seems highly unlikely, and according to Millwall fans, it is absurdly out of touch with reality (they had the balls to shoot two sequels to this film). Pre-arranged fights were not the norm amongst hooligans in the past, according to, well, hooligan firms. They didn't want to lose the spontaneity of a good fight (what a code of ethics!). They allegedly wouldn't attack 'civilian' supporters either (even if 'firms' is a slang term for criminal gangs). The 2005 movie focused primarily on the West Ham hooligans, with Millwall fans being the antagonists due to the real-life football rivalry between the clubs. In other words, Millwall fans are the villains.

Like everyone else, I had bought into my fair share of stereotypes about Millwall. If one is not from England, there is nothing else one can know about the club other than its fan base's bad reputation. Other works of fiction back that up that idea like *The Firm*, the 1989 cult classic by the influential director Alan Clarke starring a young Gary Oldman (again, Millwall hooligans are portrayed as the villains). The main problem is that *Green Street* had already oversaturated the genre of hooliganism after the release of *The Football Factory* (2004). Both films even ridiculously share an identical scene, where a group of supporters (from West Ham in the first, and Chelsea in the latter) are seen following an FA Cup draw on TV and are thrilled to learn who their teams are drawn against. 'It's fucking Millwall!' a character says.

A small club from south London became sort of the face of hooliganism. 'The glory comes not from the team, but from the reputation of the supporters,' says the narrator on the BBC's *Panorama* in 1977. The production was literally invited into the club to show the hooligan reputation was a myth. 'A good game of football, a good punch-up, a good piss-up, that is all about Millwall,' says Harry the Dog, a supporter linked to the Millwall Bushwackers, arguably one of the most feared (and hated) hooligan firms of its era in the 1970s (Harry is now dead after succumbing to drinking problems). In all fairness, though, some Millwall fans were hooligans before hooliganism even became a thing. In 1967 a referee was attacked and claimed to have been knocked unconscious after a match against Aston Villa.

However, it was the BBC documentary that changed Millwall's ethos forever. Myth and reality intersected four months after the broadcast, when a riot broke out at The Den during an FA Cup quarter-final versus Ipswich Town in March 1978. Ipswich's manager Bobby Robson would famously say that the police 'should have turned the flamethrowers on them'. The 1985 Luton riot became another low point in football hooliganism, when Millwall fans travelling for an FA Cup match against Luton Town interrupted the game several times, ripped seats from the stands, and invaded the pitch after the final whistle. From that day on, Millwall supporters would be – falsely or not – accused of violence, vandalism and 'everything bad in football'.

One might argue that the turmoil was only a reflection of what was going on in England in the 1980s, rather than being specifically related to Millwall (unemployment soared, and reached a staggering 11.9 per cent in 1984). Following the battle in Luton later in 1985, for instance, there were riots in Brixton and Tottenham's Broadwater

Farm estate. Hooliganism and socio-economic violence went hand in hand, and the majority of Millwall fans were from a working-class background heavily affected by the recession. The Heysel Stadium disaster is another low point from 1985, when Liverpool supporters charged at Juventus fans, pressing them against a collapsing wall, resulting in 39 deaths. The tragedy in Brussels caused the ban of English clubs from European competitions for five years. Millwall's reputation for violence is not entirely without reason, but if it makes them feel better, at least their actions were never responsible for banning their entire country from playing abroad.

Alex Melnikov, 16, had absolutely no part in any of this. I wanted to speak with a Millwall fan disconnected from the old times of punch-ups, as much as possible. I read several books written by former hooligans, including some by Millwall fans, and they never seemed to have lost a fight. Especially in a city like London, crowded with rich clubs and big stadiums, I wanted to talk to a youngster who deliberately chose to support a bad team. 'I can't remember the year, but my first game was a 0-0 against our local rivals Charlton, and even with the lack of goals, the atmosphere was amazing, nothing like the Premier League games you see on TV,' he says. 'The noise in the stadium was deafening. I knew from then this was what football was supposed to be like.'

Football was always an extension of the community, so it made sense to support a local club, especially in England. However, the loyalties in London are completely different now because of access to football on TV and video games. Teenagers are more likely to support a team that actually wins trophies – it is easier to find a Liverpool or Manchester United supporter in London than a Millwall fan. 'Supporting my local team has given me an experience that fans of big teams like Arsenal and Chelsea will never have,' Alex says. 'Especially with being able to go and watch my team week in, week out. Also, the lows of supporting a lower-league team make the good times mean so much more than for a supporter of a big club.' He studies in a school two blocks away from the stadium. There are only two Millwall fans in his entire class.

In London, there aren't many teams that have moved around quite as much as Millwall. They were founded at the Isle of Dogs in East London, a peninsula that includes Millwall. The club moved south of the River Thames in 1910, and retained the name despite not having played in that area for more than 100 years. The Den stadium is now in the south-east London area of Bermondsey, from where many fans left. 'Almost all fans have some connection to south London, whether it be that they moved out due to gentrification, or that their family is from that area,' Alex says. 'Our support is mostly from family tradition, rather than being from the local area now. A lot of our fans are from outside of London in Kent [where many London dockers relocated]. Some like me support [them] because it's the local team, but there are not many.'

English radio personality Danny Baker has his fandom built on his family tradition. 'My grandfather watched Millwall in their first incarnation, when they played at the Isle of Dogs. My dad was born in Millwall, raised in Millwall and worked on the Millwall docks, so he could hardly have been more Millwall had he been named "Millwall",' he writes.[14] Nevertheless, inner-city populations change, and Bermondsey (and its surrounding areas of New Cross and Deptford) faced huge transformation. In the 1970s, traditional industries closed down and there was a loss of local work. Big tower blocks were built largely for council estates and a large black community moved in. The region switched and many supporters left the area. However, the demographic of the Millwall fan hasn't changed as much: it is the white proletarian male.

Recently Bermondsey has been cited by estate agents as 'up and coming', with Georgian terraces facing either housing flats, or high-end apartments. The city council have been trying for years to purchase the area around the Millwall ground in order to sell it to an offshore property investor. The idea, naturally, is to build luxury apartments in a sports village type of redevelopment in the land currently occupied by the club's car park and the Millwall Community Trust, meaning that Millwall FC could be forced to relocate. As it is today, around The Den there is a secluded area adjacent to the railway tracks. There is also a tunnel under the rail track with an iconic graffiti mural of former striker Neil Harris, with his arms wide open. There are no pubs close to the stadium, in case one fancies a pint with an older generation hooligan. There is the Millwall Cafe instead, right across from the stadium, a family restaurant with its homemade-cooking style, serving steak and kidney pie and fish 'n' chips.

On the street facing the stadium, there are 12 auto repair shops (yes, I counted), and it is not the sort of place

---

14   Baker, D; Lineker, G., *Behind Closed Doors: Life, Laughs and Football* (London: Century, 2019)

a tourist would like to hang around, not because it is a necessarily dangerous place or anything, but instead just a typical south London working-class area. The Lions Store, Millwall's official merchandise outlet, is right beside the box office. That 'mechanics' strip' also connects to a footpath that runs parallel to the train lines directly from the train station to the stadium's away section (only used for matchdays). It was strategically designed to keep the visitors' supporters away from the Millwall fans' sight, and is surrounded by a metal fence (routinely referred to as 'Cowards' Way' by the Millwall fans). It is hard to change a reputation overnight, especially a bad one. Contrary to the lack of importance (or red alarms) of that particular game against Peterborough, I've never seen as many policemen come out as I did that evening (and I've certainly never seen so many policemen for a third division game).

According to the BBC documentary *Football Fight Club*, from 2014, it costs an estimated £25m a year to police football matches in London, and only half of the costs are covered by clubs. In the capital alone, 18,000 officers were deployed for Premier League matches in 2014. Of course, many firms remain active, but the encounters with rival firms these days are mostly organised online (unlike in the past, pre-arranged fights are trending now). The classic hooliganism, per se, was in steep decline after the Taylor Report, a series of regulations about safety at stadiums after the Hillsborough disaster in April 1989, when 96 fans died and 766 were injured due to overcrowding in the stands in Sheffield (which also coincided with the foundation of an explicitly elitist English Premier League two years later).

The New Den, opened in 1993 less than 2km from the original stadium, was the first English stadium built under the safety recommendations. All-seated stands replaced terraces and all perimeter fencing was excluded. It was deliberately designed to control Millwall supporters, with its wide corners to facilitate police access, and CCTV cameras everywhere. It was not unusual for undercover agents to sit amongst fans.

Fast-forward to a foggy Tuesday evening 25 years later, football-related arrests have declined and pitch incursions are practically non-existent these days (I was not even frisked upon entering the gates). It doesn't mean that Millwall supporters became lords. Two lads standing closer to the pitch against the wall spent the entire match cursing and taunting the referee and any opponent who dared to walk in front of them. I could not help but notice the irony of a sign saying 'It is a Criminal Offence to Use Foul or Abusive Language' right below them. I watched the game from the Dockers Stand, named in honour of the club's working-class fan base. The docks are inherently tattooed on to the fans' bodies. 'That image of a hard-working, hard-drinking, hard-fighting, hard-man bred from a life on the docks has unquestionably been passed down the generations,' Andrew Woods writes in his hooligan-type memoir.[15]

Millwall supporters are unsatisfied by nature. They hassled their opponents, their own players, the referee, the visiting Peterborough supporters and the universe. They were really angry no matter what was happening on the field. It gives them a sense of pride, I only assume. It

---

15 Woods, A., *No One Likes Us, We Don't Care: True Stories from Millwall, Britain's Most Notorious Football Hooligans* (London: John Blake Publishing, 2011)

becomes pure entertainment to observe, because if we're being honest here, the match was subpar. All that fury was the opposite experience from a night earlier in St. Pauli. Ultras, chants and activism are great, but a grumpy old fella with a cockney accent is priceless.

All the polished stadiums in English football came with a cost, naturally. I had to pay £26 for a third division match ticket, the highest price in the trip. 'This is absolutely surreal to say the least,' Alex says. 'How can we possibly pay for this every week? It is virtually impossible, especially for a student like me. We have a small fan base and our team is frequently shite. We're not in the Premier League and the results matter if people will have to pay that kind of money.' With a capacity of 20,000, The Den was less than half-full.

The average price of a ticket across the four leagues in England is nearly four times as much than in Germany, where I never paid more than €15 to watch a game (around £12.50). It is so unreally expensive that Millwall adult fans pay £350 for a season ticket, when by comparison, season tickets to watch multi-champions Bayern Munich start from just £110 (I pay close to £165 for a season ticket to watch my team in Brazil, which I already considered too much). 'They ruined the football experience in England with the expensive tickets and the all-seated stadiums,' Alex says. 'All the small clubs need to follow a certain Premier League standard, which is absurd. Chelsea's fan base has been priced out because English football is for the tourists now.' While I totally agree with Alex, it is ironic because he never actually experienced the *good old times*. He is even younger than the Taylor Report! He grew up attending a new era of modern overpriced football, where the half-time salty pie costs £4.50!

The Den resembles an old-fashioned ground, but there's no going back to the old ways. The game has pre-match build-up songs through the sound system, goal music ('Let 'Em Come' by Roy Green) and a jumbotron. Nothing like the original, sinister Den from Thatcher's era, as described by Simon Inglis in his classic book about English football stadiums.[16] 'Cold Blow Lane on a dark, wet night might be the perfect setting for a Jack the Ripper horror film: dry ice wafting about the cobbled streets and under the low tunnels.'

During the match I also had a chance to speak with Alex's friend, Jack, a shy and astonishingly British-looking young lad: white pale skin, blue eyes and crooked teeth. Supporting Millwall for him was barely a choice, as his family have supported Millwall for a few generations, and a couple of his uncles have even played for the club, one making the first team at one point. Being taken to games at a young age, his football club was predestined. I asked him about winning titles after being taken over by a foreign billionaire, such as at Chelsea and Manchester City. 'Football is for the fans and if in order to win a championship that would mean that the real fans are left out, then what is the point?' he says. 'We'd like to win titles, of course, but only if the club could maintain its status. But that's impossible, and I'd rather support Millwall on how it actually is.'

A community club is what Millwall actually is, relying almost exclusively on loyalty. The club is not building a

16 Inglis, S., *Football Grounds of England and Wales* (London: Harper Collins, 1983)

global brand, but effectively trying to build a fan base in their own backyard. Hooliganism has been perpetuated through films, documentaries and books, although what you actually see in the stadium are a large number of dads and sons as opposed to Harry the Dog, Billy the Wolf or Bobby the Butcher. There is also a surprising number of youngsters like Alex and Jack. Every conversation I had, Millwall fans told me that they're part of a family club. It seems like a very dysfunctional family, but a family nonetheless.

It is really a tiny club on the pitch with a big reputation off the pitch. In London alone, nine other clubs have had better average attendances than Millwall in the last decade. The club spent only two seasons in the English first division (the glorious 1989/90 and 1990/91), considerably less than its south-east London counterparts of Charlton (26 seasons) and Crystal Palace (19 seasons). Millwall's biggest trophies are second, third and fourth divisions, and a few appearances at Wembley. 'I'm not too sure whether I'd want Millwall to become a Premier League club, as I think we'd lose what makes our support and team special if we did,' Alex says. 'However, it would be a shame to never experience what competing at the top level is like.'

Millwall had a *Cinderella* run of top-level football when they reached the FA Cup Final in 2004, defeated 3-0 by the Manchester United of Ronaldo, Ryan Giggs and Paul Scholes (Alex was only three years old then). A week after my first visit to The Den, Millwall would have another crack at it, taking on Tottenham in the FA Cup quarter-final. 'Any chance of winning?' I ask Jack. 'None,' he says, with straightforward honesty. 'Unless everything goes our way on that day.' Spurs ended up winning 6-0, quickly reminding Millwall fans of their lower status. That is why all the 1-0 victories against all the Tranmere Rovers of the world are the most important.

The club may not have a room full of trophies, but they impose respect when it comes to the local derbies in their own region. Millwall has a head-to-head advantage against both Charlton (52 vs 45) and Crystal Palace (41 vs 25), even if it is more like a geographical rivalry for Millwall fans, where they celebrate but don't care as much about those derbies as their opponents do. Charlton and Palace fans really hate Millwall, but well, when it comes to what other London fan bases think about the club, it is really simple: *everyone hates Millwall.*

'No one likes us, we don't care' became the club's motto in the 1980s, when fans started singing the verses at stadiums to the tune of 'Sailing' by Rod Stewart – it is amusing how such a cheesy tune somehow has become a hooligan anthem. The song was a reaction to their negative press. 'Please God, don't let Millwall win promotion' ran a *Daily Mirror* headline in 1988 following a brawl at Highbury stadium against Arsenal (the newspaper even reported that Millwall supporters had plans to steal the stadium clock!). Millwall *did* win promotion that season, and to be hated by other fan bases in London became a pastime for the fans.

'Animals!' was the headline published by *The Sun* after the 1985 Luton riot; but *The Sun* also falsely blamed Liverpool supporters for the Hillsborough disaster (reports attributed the tragedy to mistakes by the police and the tabloid is boycotted by Liverpool fans up to this day). Millwall fans believe that they're badly portrayed by the media, an exaggeration more than a complete fabrication. 'While there are some obviously bad events related to our supporters recently, most media stories exaggerate events which aren't unusual at any other club just because it's us,' Alex says. 'Any little incident gets reported on if we're involved, unlike other clubs.'

Whether everyone hates Millwall, they only hate West Ham, which is arguably the fiercest rivalry in the city, even if the two clubs haven't shared the same area for more than a century now (when Millwall moved south in 1910 the so-called Dockers derby technically ended). Of course, both fan bases were made up of the dock workers, but Millwall and West Ham rarely play each other, just 39 times since World War I. The rivalry is nowadays based solely on hooliganism.

The violence is traced back to a 1972 testimonial game of Millwall's iconic defender Harry Cripps, when their firms clashed inside and outside the ground. Four years later, a Millwall fan died after falling out of a train during a fight with West Ham fans. 'West Ham boys, we've got brains, we throw Millwall under trains' was chanted in their stands after the incident. In 1986 a West Ham fan was reportedly stabbed to death. The clashes became sporadic during the height of hooliganism in the 1980s due to Millwall's poor performance (over four decades the sides were only in the same tier of the Football League for three seasons). However, they were drawn against each other in the League Cup in 2009 (just like in those silly movies!), and the match exploded into chaos before, during and after the game, and resulted in multiple pitch invasions – West Ham won the game, although I'm not sure if they do care about that.

This almost fashionista appeal to violence was also perpetuated by London gangsters from the 1960s. 'It's like the Krays versus the Richardsons, with West Ham being the Krays, the media-hungry, star-struck celebrity seekers. We were Millwall's faceless hooligans, the Richardsons, getting on with the job and trying to avoid the glare of notoriety,' Andrew Woods writes in his hooligan memoir. West Ham's owner David Sullivan financed a film about the Kray twins (which afterwards he allegedly paid people to write good reviews about).

On the pitch, West Ham are incontestably more successful. They're not global giants, but they're giants compared to Millwall: West Ham have won three FA Cup trophies, and the 1965 European Cup Winners' Cup (when they beat 1860 Munich in the final, as I mentioned earlier in this book). The club have spent 64 seasons in the top flight, and they recently moved to a 60,000-seat stadium, constructed for the 2012 Summer Olympics. West Ham had legendary players like Bobby Moore and Geoff Hurst, the only man to score a hat-trick in a World Cup Final. As for Millwall results, well, no one likes them and they don't care.

However, trophies don't play the game and Millwall dominate the head-to-head derby. They have beaten West Ham 38 times vs 34 in 99 matches (as of 2020), including the first game at The Den in 1912 (5-1) and the last one in 1992 (2-1). Also 'The Mother's Day Massacre', when Millwall won 4-1 in the first derby played at the New Den in 2004 (a massacre related to the score of the game, and not violence? That's great lads, keep up the good work). After West Ham moved even further away from Millwall, the rivalry remains only due to its historic grudge. Alex lives in Bermondsey and hasn't really met any West Ham fans. 'It's sad to see what's become of their club since moving stadiums,' he says. 'They don't seem like the same team anymore; the corporate rebranding has ruined what made them our rivals, which is a shame.'

Hooliganism was organised around fighting and drinking, but unlike the ultras culture in other parts of European football (and in South American games, where the word 'ultras' is not used), English fans don't chant for the whole game. Every team has a couple of traditional chants, but what makes them really unique are the off-the-cuff insults. When Peterborough striker Marcus Maddison packed his nose with cotton because it was bleeding, the crowd started chanting 'the tampon is not gonna stop the bleeding of your nose'. Visiting fans sat in the North Stand upper tier, as far away as possible from Millwall fans, who kept chanting 'there is a wanker in the rain, he's gonna wank in the rain' towards them (and I was amused by the fact that it was not even raining!). It was a celebration of slapstick, mediocre insults, like a profane version of *Just for Laughs*, and especially British if one calls you a wanker. However, when you think about it, it's better being insulted like this than getting a brick smashed on your head.

Not even Millwall players are immune from hurling abuse, sometimes more than the opposition. Before half-time, Fred Onyedinma, 20, was having a hard evening, sneered at, called 'fuckin' lazy', 'fuckin' shite' and such – his performance was indeed very poor. 'This is normal and the players have to be tough to play for us,' Alex says. 'Being a footballer doesn't make you necessarily a Millwall footballer. It is a subtle difference that they need to learn quickly.' The young player in question is black, and Millwall fans have been constantly labelled as racists, which they emphatically deny. Jimmy Abdou, a black Muslim former player, has been elected twice as the player of the year voted by Millwall fans, they say. Most fans were well behaved at The Den, and to be clear, at least at that particular match, I didn't hear any overt racist insults (although repeatedly calling a black player lazy may fall into covert racism).

Without commending it, I perfectly understand all the intimidation, to be honest. People normally associate Brazilian football with fun, passion and dribble-skilled players, but Brazilian football fan bases are something entirely different: the supporters are quite vocal and extremely critical of our players, sometimes leading to violence. It is definitely not unusual in football fan culture to shout insults; however, a couple of weeks before my arrival in London, Leicester made an official complaint to the FA against Millwall because of the 'abuse, provocation and intimidation' that their players and staff suffered during a loss at The Den during an FA Cup match. 'This is the absurdity that English football has become,' Alex says. 'A team complaining about cursing in a football game – is that really serious?' It is really absurd for a Millwall supporter. Upon their 1-0 victory against Peterborough following a mediocre game of football, many supporters left the stadium whining about their performance. Millwall had just completed 16 games without losing.

Of course, not everything at the stadium is about insults. They celebrated Ben Thompson, 21, a young midfielder who had played his entire career for Millwall, coming from a family of supporters. 'He is one of our own,' they chanted, to the tune 'Sloop John B' by The Beach Boys. Their head coach Neil Harris is the man pictured on the graffiti mural in the tunnel leading to the stadium, a Millwall legend, the club's top scorer, with 138 goals. Whereas the lower leagues in England are dominated by short-term contracts, half of the Millwall players on the pitch had been there for more than two years. You might be a shite player, but you gotta be loyal to the team.

At the end of the day, Millwall fans like being labelled 'The Most Hated in England'. Myth and reality are interfused all the time, such as the story of Millwall fan Roy Larner during the London Bridge terrorism attack later that year. The 47-year-old man reportedly fought three knife-wielding attackers with his fists, while shouting 'Fuck off! I'm Millwall'. He was hospitalised with a total of eight stab wounds to the head, chest and hands. 'I didn't think of my safety at the time. I'd had four or five pints – nothing major,' he told *The Guardian*. Larner was unemployed and living on a friend's sofa, just a regular tough, ageing, white Millwall supporter. TV presenter Piers Morgan said on his show: 'Millwall fans get a very bad rap, a lot of it very deserved, but there are times when you really want a lot of Millwall fans, and that was one of them.'

Midweek games tend to have a flatter atmosphere than the Saturday ones, but all the fame of violence and hooliganism made no sense, after watching Millwall at the stadium. A third division match on a winter night did not strike me as the atmosphere that made Alex fall in love with his local football club. On our way out, there were no screams, kicks or bottles thrown, or any confrontation with the 'Old Bill', even though the policemen were still there as if prepared for a battle. Millwall fans try too hard for people not to like them, but it didn't work on me.

As generations of their fans have watched decades of mediocre football punctuated by little moments of success (and they don't care!), Millwall finished the 2016/17 season playing in the promotion play-offs at Wembley for the second consecutive year. They eventually got promoted to the Championship (second division) after beating Bradford 1-0 with five minutes left on the clock, in front of 53,000 fans. At the end of the game, Millwall fans invaded the pitch to celebrate the victory and promotion. The police made 12 arrests. No one likes them.

Next stop: Glasgow, Scotland
Distance: 663km (412 miles)
How to get there: Nine hours and 50 minutes by bus
The best advice: Taking a bus to Glasgow is probably not good advice, but it is cheaper than spending a night in London, so I recommend booking an overnight bus. Ha!
Soundtrack: 'Guns of Brixton' by The Clash

CHAPTER 7

THE LAST KINGS
OF SCOTLAND

Queen's Park FC 1-1 Livingston
Hampden Park
Saturday, 4 March 2017
Scottish League One (Third Division)
Attendance: 701

It wouldn't make much sense to go to Scotland for the weekend with the sole purpose of watching a third division game with 700 people in a stadium that holds 52,000. However, that is precisely what I did. 'If you're going to try, go all the way. Otherwise, don't even start,' Charles Bukowski once wrote, although if I had to guess, he was not talking about visiting a small football club from Glasgow. I could've stayed in south London, as originally planned, to cover AFC Wimbledon, a club founded by the fans after their original team relocated to Milton Keynes and changed their name to MK Dons; a second option was a shorter trip to Manchester to see FC United of Manchester, also founded by supporters discontent with the takeover of Manchester United by an American businessman. So keep that in mind: this is not Queens Park Rangers from London, but Queen's Park FC from Glasgow.

It wouldn't make much sense to go to Scotland for the weekend, but not only that, I made the trip by bus, which took nine hours! The coach left London on a Friday at 8am with four stops in Milton Keynes (oh really?), Norton Canes (a service station in the middle of absolutely nowhere), Manchester (I should've got off!) and Carlisle. I had a lot of time to think 'what the hell am I doing here?' Trust me, I really did ask myself this question. However, the bus station in Carlisle is right next to Brunton Park (the largest English stadium with terraces!), so I also got myself thinking about the possibility of making a quick stop there on my way back. 'This could mean losing girlfriends, relatives and maybe even your mind. It could mean derision. It could mean mockery – isolation. And, you'll do it, despite rejection and the worst odds,' Bukowski resumed, in that very same book. Nah, not this time, Charlie. I quickly abandoned the idea.

Let's be clear here, Queen's Park FC is a football institution. Founded in 1867, they are the oldest club in Scotland and they were celebrating the club's 150th anniversary. The club was wearing the navy blue jersey to celebrate, the one currently associated with the Scottish national team, but originally worn by the club. In the world's first-ever international friendly game, when Scotland took on England in 1872, all the players representing the Scottish side played for Queen's Park. Since then, they have adopted the white and black jersey in horizontal stripes, their colours to this day, giving rise to their nickname 'The Spiders'.

Queen's Park's legacy of football is even extended to how the game is played. In the first years of football, players would run with the ball until they were brought down (a rudimentary version of rugby). It was at Queen's Park that the 'passing game' was introduced, as famously described by Jonathan Wilson in his encyclopedic book about football tactics.[17] Recent descriptions would suggest they were 'the Barcelona of the 19th century', 'the inventors of tiki-taka', amongst other hideous definitions. Queen's Park allegedly changed football rules too: they introduced half-time to games and free kicks. It hasn't yet been officially recognised by FIFA.

Furthermore, Queen's Park was the most popular team in Glasgow. They won ten Scottish Cup titles (fewer only than Rangers and Celtic, even today). The team was led by its defender Andrew Watson, the first black player to play football in Scotland and to win a major competition (he later moved to London to become the first black footballer to play in the FA Cup). For those first 20 years between 1870 and 1890, Queen's Park was Scotland's football driving force. At the turn of the century, however, the club refused to participate in the Scottish League, where footballers were paid salaries. Queen's Park remains to this day an amateur club.

If today many football fans are 'against modern football', Queen's Park have been against it for over 100 years. Their squad of players is unpaid, therefore the club can maintain its original amateur status and uphold 'the purity of sports'. To be precise: Queen's Park play professional competitions (they are currently in the third division), but their athletes are considered amateurs: the club doesn't pay wages nor

---

17   Wilson, J., *Inverting the Pyramid: The History of Football Tactics* (London: Orion, 2008)

do they buy or sell players. The club wants to do justice to its motto of *Ludere Causa Ludendi*: to play for the sake of playing.

However, as one can imagine, it is very hard to compete at the highest level just for the sake of playing; 125 years after Queen's Park's last Scottish Cup title, the two hegemonic teams in Glasgow are obviously Rangers and Celtic (the Old Firm). In the first two decades of the professional league only, Rangers won ten national leagues and Celtic another ten (as of February 2021 they have won 54 and 51, respectively). The last time Queen's Park took part in the first division was in the 1957/58 season, when they were relegated with 29 losses over 34 matches, conceding a record-breaking 114 goals in the campaign.

Queen's Park is run by a committee and staffed by volunteers; and I wanted to understand better how it manages an amateur side in a professional league. I was received by the club's commercial director, Garry Templeman, who has been a board member for the team since 1999, and works as a corporate manager for a bank. I quickly realised he was giving me a guided tour through Hampden Park stadium. I visited its dressing rooms, press room, the equipment room, where I was introduced to someone preparing the team's gear for the game, and the underground parking (which, according to Garry, introduced a pattern to all stadiums in Europe). He took me to the pitch and I was impressed by the shiny green grass.

Hampden Park has been Scotland's national stadium since 1906. It holds the European record for the highest attendance at a club game, set in 1937 when more than 147,000 people showed up for the Scottish Cup Final. The stadium has been renovated: it is monumental and modern, one of the best in Europe, a UEFA category four stadium (the highest standard). Three UEFA Champions League Finals were played at Hampden, including the one with the unforgettable volley by Zinedine Zidane when Real Madrid beat Bayer Leverkusen in 2002.

Queen's Park is the stadium's owner, and it is almost hard to believe, especially considering an illogical average crowd of 540 in a stadium for 52,000. Upon renovating the stadium in 1997, the Scottish Football Association (SFA) became the sole administrator until 2020 as part of the leasing agreement, renewable for another 20 years. What the SFA basically does with the stadium is whatever they want, provided they pay the rent to Queen's Park. 'To comply with the new rules of security imposed by the SFA itself, our club was forced to carry out a big renovation in the 1990s, and our debts rose,' Garry explains. 'It was no fault of our own, and we made an agreement with the SFA for tenancy, providing they paid for the renovation. The club survived [its financial debts] and is now seeing every cent of that business.'

The SFA pays £300,000 annually for the rental, according to sources, accounting for almost half of Queen's Park's £750,000 revenue each season – the average salary budget for players between Rangers and Celtic is nearly 50 times higher, according to the UEFA Benchmark Report from January 2019. Queen's Park also owns the adjacent Lesser Hampden, a stadium with a 470 capacity, used as a training facility for the first team, and hosts the games of the youth teams. The dressing rooms building, a converted farmhouse which dates back to the 19th century, is believed to be the oldest existing football stadium building in the world.

With the big pay cheque received every month, Garry estimates that the club needs around 600 fans per game for Queen's Park not to lose money. The club needs its revenue for maintenance and to pay staff, like the 37 stewards hired every game for security (which honestly seemed unnecessary). Why do they play in a giant stadium like this? 'It is our stadium and it is where we've played for over 100 years now,' Garry says. The club used to have a larger fan base until the early 1940s, which dramatically dropped to four figures in the 1970s, and eventually reached its current numbers of less than 1,000 fans per game.

'We are just a few, but like no other,' says Keith McAllister, a Queen's Park supporter who reportedly hasn't missed a match home or away since 1979 (when he was 21). This is what he does on Saturdays, he says, casually, despite the fact that he's seen about 1,900 official matches since a young age. Keith doesn't consider himself a superfan and neither is he trying to break any records. 'It would be quite a strange record to hold, but I have watched games since I was seven; the number has obviously piled up,' he says. He hopes that Queen's Park never concedes to football professionalism because this is what he thinks makes the club special. 'It would become just another football club, and there is nothing special about that.'

Amateurism is a badge of honour for Queen's Park fans, or as they like to say, it is *real* football. People who love football normally play football for fun and think that the club being amateur approximates the fans with the sport's roots. They emphatically care about winning and the league, but they believe football somehow represents life, where expectations sometimes are not fulfilled. They are aware that Queen's Park will never win a big trophy, so they celebrate the small ones as if they were UEFA Champions Leagues. The third division-winning season in 1980/81 is Keith McAllister's favourite, when Queen's Park was promoted to the Scottish second tier before they started bouncing between third and fourth divisions since then.

Keith is a tall 59-year-old man with glasses, grey hair and a Van Dyke-style goatee. He's the secretary of the QP Supporters' Association and works in the souvenir shop before kick-off at home matches. He cares about the fans as much as he cares about the club. It was him that arranged my press pass, took me to the supporters' club bar after the game and introduced me to other supporters and his friends. He does de facto PR for Queen's Park, and contrary to what his devotion may suggest, he's modest and sharp as a whip, with no self-importance.

He's a devoted Scotsman as well, following Tartan Army wherever they play, home and abroad, wearing his kilt and the whole regalia (it would be accurate to say that Hampden is his second home). Keith has a Hugh MacDiarmid poem from 1931 tattooed on his arm, a reflection of his love for Scotland and for Queen's Park: 'The rose of all the world is not for me; I want for my part; Only the little white rose of Scotland; That smells sharp and sweet – and breaks the heart.' On his leg, he has tattooed the crest of Wattenscheid 09, a German football club from Bochum who currently play in Germany's fifth division, and with whom Queen's Park fans somehow have become associated.

Amongst many Scots football fans (especially Celtic and Rangers), there is a disaffection towards Hampden Park. The seats are far from the action, and many fans consider it has a neutral atmosphere for Scotland's international games. However, the sectarianism in Glasgow surrounding Celtic and Rangers has always prevented the national team playing somewhere else. The SFA have been meaning to buy the stadium for good, which would probably lead Queen's Park to find another home. 'We are no longer at the top, but we are not as recognised as we should be,' says McAllister. 'We've done more than any other [team] for the game's history, but our contribution is under-appreciated, which is a shame.'

Scotland has not qualified for the World Cup since 1998, so Hampden became a scapegoat for the nation's failure. If somehow a packed 52,000-seat stadium lacks atmosphere, according to some fans, try to imagine it with only 700 seats occupied. Only a fifth of the stadium is actually open to the public during Queen's Park matches. Everyone is crammed into the centre pavilion, while visiting fans spread themselves across three or four rows without any physical barriers, only a half dozen stewards (for there is absolutely no need for them).

It was a cold afternoon on the day I visited and the weather report said it was about to rain. But it is always cold and about to rain in Glasgow. The average fan was either a senior or a child. I guess you've got to be very young before you fully understand the implication of supporting such team, either that or very advanced in years and therefore too far off in life to give up. The sound on the pitch was vivid from players kicking the ball, screaming at each other or the head coach shouting instructions and the fans cursing. 'That's why your wifey hates ya, you bampot,' shouts an elderly man at the referee (or in other non-Scottish words, 'you idiot'). The insults seem personal like they know the guy, and perhaps they do.

In the Queen's Park social media photos, there are always the same people in the stands (I was introduced to the club's photographer, Ian Cairns). The atmosphere is effectively non-existent, which is a little eccentric for outsiders. Occasionally, I could hear a 'mon the Spiders!' being shouted, but never a coordinated chant. The fan base exploded only once in 90 minutes, when Queen's Park tied the game, immediately suffocated by the song 'Enjoy Yourself' by The Specials (even if I'm truly not a fan of goal music, I have to say that if you're gonna pick a song, pick it right, like Queen's Park). 'Enjoy yourself, it's later than you think.'

The vibrant green grass contrasted with the poor quality of football, the typical kick-and-rush lower-league game, essentially made of long balls and very physical. The opposite style of the 'inventors of the passing style' that Queen's Park became famous for nearly a century before. Queen's Park's goal was a beauty, though, after 19-year-old striker Dario Zanatta passed a defender before hitting a right-footed cannon into the top-left corner. Livingston scored earlier in a proper Scotland manner: a header following a set-piece situation. Results will always prevail over aesthetics when you don't have bags of money to buy Neymars and Mbappés.

Queen's Park is the only amateur club in Scotland playing in a professional league. Most players receive their 'wages' in the form of expenses, such as football gear. They sign a contract of £1 per week in order to comply with the labour laws in the United Kingdom (others were playing for Queen's Park on loan, like Canadian-born Zanatta from Heart of Midlothian). Garry Templeman explained that many players choose to play for Queen's Park because of Hampden Park. 'Our philosophy does not allow us to pay wages, but our infrastructure, you won't find in other clubs, even clubs in the Premiership [first division],' he says. 'It is a dream for almost every professional footballer in Scotland to play at the national stadium.'

Recently, Queen's Park members voted to allow ex-professionals to be hired, provided the transfer is free of charge (expired contracts, loans, etc.). The team won the promotion play-offs in the 2015/16 season to go up to the third division, and finished the 2016/17 season very close to the promotion play-offs to the second tier. 'So near, and yet so far,' wrote Keith McAllister by email, later that season. Most players are youngsters looking for playing time.

Ryan McGeever, 23 and 6ft 3in, looks like a typical Scottish defender more than one might expect from a typical Scottish defender. He started at the club aged 16, left to play for other teams, and came back following a couple of injuries in his career. 'The advantage of playing for a professional team is being able to focus on football only,' he says. 'But here at Queen's Park, because everyone has to work [in regular jobs], we only have a chance to practise six hours every week. This requires a lot of teamwork, and we need to work harder on that short period.' Ryan is studying to become a physical education teacher.

The club became a point of entry for many lads aspiring to become footballers. Scotland's captain Andy Robertson reached Queen's Park at 18, dumped by Celtic as a junior after being told that 'he was too wee' (he's 5ft 10in, which is my height). After a remarkable season, he transferred to the Premiership's Dundee United, then Hull City and eventually Liverpool. McGeever has similar aspirations and returned to Glasgow to complete his university degree. 'My desire is to make a living from playing professional football, but when you don't get to play for the Premiership teams, then it makes it very difficult to build your career out of it,' he says. 'We must have an alternative plan.' The defender was selected for the Team of the Year at the end of the season and signed for second division Brechin City. A lack of compensation for players makes it almost impossible to protect the club from losing their top players free of charge.

At half-time, Garry Templeman took me to Hampden Park's skybox, where all board members watched the game, along with guests and businessmen. I was served a pint of Tennent's Lager before I got the chance to even blink (alcohol cannot be served in football stadiums in Glasgow, with an exemption for corporate hospitality areas). After my drink, it was suggested that I tried pie and Bovril, a Scottish football tradition made of concentrated beef tea extract.

I was introduced to the *Brief History of Scottish Cuisine* at a table with a family consisting of three brothers (Alan, Tom and Gerry, all in their 60s) and one son, Thomas – a middle-aged man that I really couldn't understand with his strong Scottish accent. The son of Garry Templeman, Jeff, 24, was there and gave me a CD with a recording of the club's anthem, where he plays the trombone. Every Spider in the stadium seems to know each other and is connected to the club on some level. They offered me a can of Irn-Bru ('iron brew'), the Scottish national soft drink (a top seller in the country, outperforming Coca Cola, I was told). If I had to describe it, it tastes like a weird flavour of Fanta mixed with tonic water. The soft drink is produced in Glasgow and has sponsored the Queen's Park jersey since 1997 (Under Armour is the kit supplier, but here nobody really cares what the company's CEO thinks about Donald Trump).

Pat McGeady, 57, is also at this round table, a smiling blue-eyed man, a football encyclopedia kind of guy. He wears a Third Lanark jacket, a football club that dissolved in 1967, when he became a Queen's Park fan almost by association. Third Lanark's former ground, Cathkin Park, is a ten-minute walk from Hampden, and still exists, although completely abandoned, covered in old leaves and with moss on its terraces. If you were thinking that an entire fan base made of 700 fans was unconventional, then can you imagine supporting a team that doesn't even exist anymore? Third Lanark's superfan is the uncle of the Irish international Aiden McGeady, who started his youth career at Queen's Park aged 12 before moving on to Celtic and eventually to the English Premier League. *Everyone in the room is connected.*

The club maintains its ties with its former players, The Queensparkers. Peter Buchanan, 78, is one of the club's top goalscorers, with 160 between 1960 and 1969. 'I had a good job at the time that I wouldn't leave for a football career,' he says. 'I had offers from professional teams, but if I had broken my leg or something there was never a guarantee, so I opted to stay at my regular job while playing for Queen's Park.' He used to work for a whisky factory, and was a contemporary of Sir Alex Ferguson, who debuted for the team in 1958. 'He was just a 16-year-old boy when I returned from the army service, and he never managed to establish himself as a starter and preferred to leave,' Buchanan says. 'I scored more goals than him,' he jokes, before telling me he has the record of goals scored in a season. Once retired, Buchanan served as Queen's Park president and is a current board member.

Ross Caven, 52, spent his entire career of 20 years playing for Queen's Park. He made over 500 appearances from 1982 to 2002, a record with the club. 'On top of my gratitude for playing for this club, it was very convenient for my personal life,' he says. 'I work as a business consultant and I was required to travel many times over the years. With contractual obligations that wouldn't be possible, but has always been negotiable with Queen's Park. It worked for my career.' Caven was the team captain when they won his first and only trophy.

Can you imagine it? Footballers spending two decades with the same team is already rare, let alone the same amateur team. Before turning 18, Ross went on trials for London club Queens Park Rangers, but he couldn't make it to the first team. 'It is likely that I would have stayed if they had accepted me,' he says. 'But the truth is that football has never seduced me as much as for the other lads, and I started thinking about another career from an early age.'

I asked him about the financial gap between the Old Firm duo of Celtic and Rangers in relation to all the other Scottish teams. 'To tell you the truth, what I like about football is the competition and that is what the smaller leagues have always given me,' he says. 'I understand the financial aspect of football and all that, but when you look at the [Premiership] table and see Celtic 30 points ahead of second place, this is not football. If that's the pathway we're heading in, I think fans will quickly realise that it is not attractive. They might stop coming to the games and it might be too late when the clubs realise it.'

[Flashback to a couple of hours before the Queen's Park game, at the Hampden lounge. There, I saw Rangers demolish Hamilton 6-0 on TV, a game I had considered seeing at the Ibrox Stadium – it would've been just a 15-minute cab ride from where I was after all. However, I wouldn't dare risk missing what I was in the city for – I'm a professional, folks!]

[Flash forward to a day after the Queen's Park game, at Celtic Park Stadium. There, I saw Celtic demolish St Mirren 4-1, a game with a semi-empty crowd of 27,000 fans, even if the tickets were sold for a promotional £20. At the box office, I just asked for 'any section with a good atmosphere', which could probably be a code for 'the worst view possible for this tourist'. Truth is that they gave me a seat in the centre in the Main Stand. My first experience at the Celtic stadium was as incredible as was possible. They know what they're doing.

I was surrounded by season-ticket holders in their 70s. Of course, the game had the ambience of a 'formality victory', since Celtic has been dominating Scottish football for years; nonetheless their fan base showed why they're considered one of the best in Europe. They celebrated and chanted loudly and harassed the opponents furiously. The old man sitting next to me was the typical 'head coach fan', all the time giving instructions to the players. He enthusiastically gave me high-fives after every Celtic goal without even knowing me. Yes, it is boring when the same team wins the title year after year, but perhaps (and only perhaps) it is not exactly boring for the supporter of the winning team. I couldn't have asked for a better atmosphere.]

Now cut back to the present day at Hampden packed with 701 fans, the second half begins; it is colder and the promised rain in Glasgow is now falling down in sheets. The game gets uglier, more aerial kicks and tackles. When I brought in my phone camera for too long, a security guard warned me that filming is forbidden, likely due to broadcasting rights – yeah right, someone is just waiting for the video highlights of a totally random Scottish third division game to be uploaded on YouTube, sure! Oh, I forgot: I was there as a journalist.

The press box was just a row in front of the fans. There were four of us. The loudspeaker announced substitutions, and it sounded like The Rolling Stones equipment being used for calling bingo numbers at nursing homes. It is quite bizarre, but Queen's Park had the fourth-*highest* average attendance in the third division, since the league average attendance that season was 559 fans per game. In absolute numbers, Queen's Park is not even the third-biggest fan base in Glasgow after the Old Firm: it is Partick Thistle, from the second division, that has become Queen's Park's natural rivals lately for sharing the division.

When, in 2012, Rangers faced liquidation and was relegated to the fourth division, Queen's Park hosted a five-figure attendance for the first time in 30 years. It only happened because the 30,000 fans at Hampden were there to support Rangers, who won 1-0. The fixture was regarded as the Original Old Firm, as the first competitive match between the two sides was in March 1879, nine years before Celtic's first match.

The last Queen's Park encounter against Celtic was in 2009 for the Scottish Cup, 117 years after Celtic's first-ever major trophy when they beat Queen's Park (Queen's Park got their revenge a year after by beating Celtic in the final of 1893, their tenth and last Scottish Cup trophy). Unlike the two giant teams of the city, Queen's Park's fan base has never identified with one political movement or religion. And unlike small clubs 'adopted' by bigger fan bases as their 'second club', the indications I've received from Rangers and Celtic fans is that they don't give a damn about Queen's Park (perhaps because they're occupied by smashing each other's skulls).

The game at Hampden finished 1-1, a good result for Queen's Park against the future champions Livingston. Anton Brady, 23, was the man of the match, and received a bottle of champagne on the pitch as his prize. After the game, I talked to head coach Gus MacPherson in the skybox room. He had changed into social attire; gone were the team's jacket and cleats that he wore on the pitch, as he continually shouted at his players like a madman. 'I was actually calm today,' he jokes. 'Demanding and passionate, this is my style.' Despite the fact he was born in Glasgow, he had no previous relationship with Queen's Park. Unlike the players and the club's committee, he is a paid employee of the club, earning an undisclosed salary (it's compatible with his peers in the Scottish third division).

'The hardest part of coaching here is that our players don't stay for long,' he says. 'Every player wants to be at a higher level, and when we are promoted like we were last season, it is normal that other clubs come after them, and they leave for a bigger team. Some decide to stay longer because they'll have more playing time here, even if they're very young.'

When Andrew Robertson left after a good third division campaign, three other players joined him in top-flight Scottish clubs at the time, including Scottish international Lawrence Shankland, who plays for Dundee United. 'We have a great environment to develop players here,' says MacPherson. 'These are the best training facilities in the country, along with Celtic and Rangers, but without the same pressure to win. We prioritise the tactical and technical aspects of their games, and we don't overload them physically. They need to adjust faster, though, since they usually stay here for a short period.' Robertson is a case of pride for the club and the fans. He had a chance to play football when no other club believed in him. While at Queen's Park he even used to work at the Hampden call centre selling tickets for concerts and events.

Gus MacPherson was in charge of the club for three years, part of a structure that rarely changes its coaches. In the past 40 years, Queen's Park has had only eight head coaches, with Eddie Hunter probably being the supporters' favourite. He coached the team from 1979 to 1994, with an impressive record of 283 losses (!) and 227 wins. Hunter also played for the club from 1964 to 1974. He was not present at the game, for some reason.

A former boss of mine worked for BBC Scotland, and after the game, I was interviewed for the radio show *Off the Ball* (which I later learned has been a Scottish football institution for the last 25 years). They asked me to describe the experience of seeing Queen's Park at Hampden. This is how I remember my answer to the question: 'It was like watching your nephew play an inter-city schools tournament at the Maracanã.'

The hosts Stuart Cosgrove and Tim Cowan then proceeded to ask me about similarities between the Scottish and Brazilian football style, and my answer was 'probably none except for the 11 players on the pitch' (hey, don't get me wrong: I was not trying to make fun of the Scottish way of playing the game, although what I saw that afternoon was definitely different from the Brazilian 'joga bonito' style). They finished the interview by asking me if I considered Pelé the best of all time. Of course I do! Even if I was Scandinavian, my answer would have been the same.

It is fascinating the admiration that Scottish fans in general have for Brazilian football, perhaps because the two countries met at three different World Cups. Pat McGeady, the encyclopedic superfan, considers Rivelino his favourite player of all time, describing details about his performance in Scotland vs Brazil in the 1974 World Cup. Roddie McVake, my former boss at the 2016 Summer Olympics in Rio, told me later that his father almost named him Júnior, after the Brazilian left-winger in the 1982 World Cup (more about Júnior later in this book). When Roddie lived in Rio de Janeiro, he once asked the former player (currently a football TV pundit) to sign his Flamengo jersey and to record a video for his father (his dad burst into tears of joy).

I stopped counting how many times somebody asked me about 'Pelé or Maradona'.

As for the Queen's Park supporters, the day is not finished after the game is finished. The match is only part of it, an excuse for their camaraderie. Keith McAllister, who has been attending Queen's Park games for almost three decades, took me to the supporter's club bar. Photos of historical players are hung on the walls, in addition to a plaque quoting Queen's Park prodigy Sir Alex Ferguson: 'If you play for Queen's Park, you have to fight every game you play.' Keith introduced me to several other Spiders: Andy, Shepa, Ian, Marty and Fergah.

'The results are secondary; of course we talk about football, we all want Queen's Park to win, but every Saturday we'll be here, no matter what the outcome,' says Andrew 'Andy' McNaught. 'The difference is that we might stay longer [at the bar] when we win.' He was interrupted by Colin Shepard, aka Shepa, a red-headed bearded man with dreadlocks wearing a bandana, saying that Andy was an old man who never could stay out late. To which Marty replied that it was easier for those without a wife, pointing directly at Shepa. Friends making fun of each other, talking about football and whatever else over loads of pints.

Ian Nicolson, a former Edinburgh Hibernian fan converted to Queen's Park, says, 'I'd rather see games in the lower leagues because of the atmosphere. It is the real football, the football closer to our reality of what we play. We watch the Premier League, Barcelona, and all, but we think Queen's Park is the kind of club that suits our personal lives.' All these guys are nine-to-five, middle-class workers and live close by. The people I spoke with at the skybox earlier in the afternoon 'are not like them', one of them made a point of saying. 'We watch the game in the stands, not at a luxurious VIP space.' Marty asked about whisky, a subject that I have zero knowledge of. After flashing me a look of complete disbelief, he served me a couple of shots of 'real whisky' from the region. I got lost in Glasgow when I left later that night.

These lads talk about anything and everything, from football to Teenage Fanclub (which they schooled me are not from Glasgow but Bellshill, 16km east), from Glasgow's terrible weather to Scotland's independence, which they were unanimously in favour of. While it doesn't mean they're more Celtic (the pro-independence Catholic fan base) than Rangers (the pro-Union Jack Protestant fan base), since sectarianism in Glasgow is precisely the reason many of these lads chose to support Queen's Park instead. 'They are stuck into an idea that doesn't have anything to do with football,' Andy says. 'Many of us are atheists so we don't care,' he laughs. When it comes to the religious animosity amongst two Glasgow superclubs, they proceed to tell me a joke: 'In the 1980s it was impossible to find a single Rangers lad at a Catholic school here. But times have changed and today is different ... you can maybe find one or two.'

The two big teams from Glasgow have played in a league of their own for decades. Queen's Park fans are not interested, and not because of some deep idealisation of being against modern football. I spent several hours with these folks, and they never sold me the idea that Queen's Park is better, or that their fan base is better. They simply don't know how to be something else. As for myself, it was a magnificent experience that had nothing to do with the game (which was horrendous), but with their passion for supporting their team – the smallest of all teams. They were not making concessions because I was there. For them, it was just another Saturday.

Next stop: London, England
Distance: 663km (412 miles)
How to get there: Nine hours and 50 minutes by bus
Best advice: Forget what I just said about saving money. Just take the train
Soundtrack: 'Enjoy Yourself' by The Specials

CHAPTER 8

NOBODY HATES FULHAM

Fulham 1-1 Leeds United
Craven Cottage
Tuesday, 7 March 2017
Championship (Second Division)
Attendance: 22,239

London is football's capital, with clubs from all walks of life, whether a local community club like Sutton United, or the nouveau riche like Chelsea, but only one is the oldest club and that's Fulham Football Club. Different postal codes give London an aspect of many cities within a city, and the rough area around The Den in the south-east is definitely not the same as the posh south-west, where attractions include Buckingham Palace, Hugh Grant and the oldest football stadium, and that's Craven Cottage of Fulham Football Club. Every team in London, stereotypically or not, is associated with a certain type of fan base: Arsenal is multicultural, Tottenham is the local Jewish, Millwall and West Ham are working-class dockers, Chelsea are ex-hooligans, and one fan base is particularly friendly and that's Fulham Football Club.

The Craven Cottage stadium is on the banks of the River Thames, a pleasant walk through a promenade along the river or by impressive Victorian houses from Hammersmith station. Either way is gorgeous and touristy, although I had a stop to make at Chancellors Pub to meet Daniel Crawford and his friends for the traditional pre-match flat pints. Crawford is a local Labour councillor and board member of the Fulham Supporters' Club, and has been a true Fulham FC fanatic since 1993. 'I was first taken to the Cottage by my neighbours, and it was a different experience from what I expected because there was no one there,' he says. 'The club was bad at the time, even losing to non-league clubs in the FA Cup. It was more like a social occasion for me, and that is what initially got me hooked. I take it more seriously now.'

Fulham beat Swansea 3-1 on that day in November 1993 with 3,000 people at the Cottage, as the team finished that season relegated to the fourth division. In the opening weeks of 1996, Fulham was 91st of the 92 clubs in the Football League, and it is part of their supporters' culture to brag about how the club was once ranked second from bottom in the entire country and ten years later was promoted to the Premier League. 'Supporting Fulham is like being on a roller coaster,' says Liam, who is at the table, a tall and corpulent, long-haired man with a sailor tattoo on his forearm. After a decade in the Premier League, Fulham is back to the second division now.

Unlike the club's darkest period, however, average home attendance increased from 4,200 fans in the 1995/96 season to nearly 20,000 only five seasons later. All matches at Craven Cottage are normally sold out these days, although it is easier to find tickets on the spot compared with other, bigger clubs in London. However, the Fulham resurrection had nothing to do with a romantic fairy tale. It came from money.

As soon as the club got its promotion to the third division in the 1990s, Fulham was bought by billionaire Harrods owner Mohamed Al-Fayed for £6.25m. With the most expensive squad outside the top two divisions, they easily got promoted to the second tier of English football (under head coach Kevin Keegan, who left the club to become manager of England). Two more years and Fulham reached the top division for the first time since 1968. It took only five years and three promotions, from the fourth to the first division, where Fulham spent 13 consecutive years. They were like a not-so-rich version of the modern nouveau riche. 'Everything quickly changes in football, and it has always been like this,' Dan Crawford says. 'Head coaches, players and owners come and go, but it is the fans that will always remain with the club, so I don't care who bought us. We enjoyed every year we spent in the Premier League knowing that without Al-Fayed, it would've been very difficult for a small club like Fulham.'

There is a common question on football forums of clubs benefitting from billionaire owners, such as Manchester City and Chelsea: *Where Were You When We Were Shit?* Nevertheless, Fulham was either not rich enough to ever make a serious title challenge, or poor enough to be instantly relegated. They finished outside the top ten in the Premier League table on nine occasions over 13 years, but were always safe. 'I've been coming here [at the stadium] since we were in the fourth division and I am still here for the Championship,' Crawford says. 'As long as they [the owners] don't change what is fundamental about our club, I don't care who's in control.'

Let's say, for the sake of argument, if the owner placed a Michael Jackson statue in front of the stadium, would that be considered fundamental? *A fuckin' statue of Michael Jackson!* Mohamed Al-Fayed was a close friend of the King of Pop, who famously attended a football match at Craven Cottage in 1999, when Fulham played Wigan while in the second division. 'He was a true genius. He had a rare gift that inspired people in every country, and he loved Fulham,' said the 81-year-old businessman during the statue unveiling. Some Fulham fans were obviously outraged, which Al-Fayed responded to by saying, during a media scrum: 'They can go to hell! I don't want them to be fans. If they don't believe in things I believe in, they can go to Chelsea, go anywhere else.'

Fulham supporters are not naturally angry, and it didn't take long for them to accept the statue (and well, they finished the season qualified for the Europa League). The fans talk about it not as if it was humiliating, but really an April Fool eccentricity from a billionaire (even if some local rivals might ask them if Madonna will be next). Al-Fayed eventually sold the club in July 2013 for £200m to Pakistani-American Shahid Khan, owner of the NFL's Jacksonville Jaguars. The new chairman immediately removed the statue, which Al-Fayed has credited as the main reason for Fulham's relegation to the second division later in the season. *Who's bad?*

The fans of Fulham were exposed early on to disappointments, so it's something they have to get used to quickly. They, in fact, talk about every accomplishment of their team like a dad bragging about the two steps his toddler son takes. 'Unless you support a mega club that plays in the [UEFA] Champions League every year, you'll never know what the season will be like,' Liam says. 'I knew that I would have to deal with losses when I chose to support Fulham, and football is attractive because you cannot predict the result. The unpredictable aspect of the game makes our daily routine less boring.' After five pints, one gets very philosophical.

From the pub to the stadium, we walked through an ocean of white shirts. The sites surrounding the ground are located in a sought-after residential area that has gradually been taken over by the upper class. When the club was near oblivion during the mid-90s, many proposals suggested redeveloping the Cottage area into a complex of luxury apartments overlooking the Thames, with a potential value of £180m, according to London estate agents Douglas & Gordon and *The Telegraph*. Fortunately, Fulham FC won the real estate battle, and currently the only thing they need to worry about is their neighbours complaining about the noise on matchdays. However, this is a matter of like it or lump it, as they say. The stadium has been there for 120 years, the oldest one in London.

As we strolled alongside the Victorian houses, Crawford was greeted by almost everyone on the way. He buys me a fanzine, *There's Only One F in Fulham*, first published by the supporters in 1988, and where he writes a column (the name is inspired by the chants of 'There's Only One Fucking Fulham' that I heard at the stadium later on). I especially liked an opinion piece written by John Clarke, a criticism of modern football, Sky, and the fan bases of the so-called big clubs. 'The TV money has ensured the "big clubs" have dominated the league which has been compounded by allowing the top four entrance to the Champions League each season ensuring that the rich get even richer. Arsène Wenger has been heavily criticised by some Arsenal fans and one can only imagine the pain they have to endure having finished in the top four [of the league] for his 20 years in charge,' he writes.

Another section of the fanzine, *Fulham: The Crap Years*, is the ultimate example of the *Fulhamish* culture, which is their fan base's ability to ridicule the team (and sometimes themselves). It is reflected more clearly when it comes to the rivalry against Chelsea. In the derby history, Fulham have only beaten Chelsea nine times. When I asked Crawford about it, he insisted on categorising it as a fierce rivalry, which made his friend Liam a little angry. 'This rivalry happens only in your mind!' he shouted. 'We spent 13 years in the Premier League and we beat Chelsea only once. Once! I wouldn't consider it a rivalry. They don't care about us.'

Even if it is a local derby from south-west London, perhaps he has a point. The clubs are separated by a 30-minute walking distance as Chelsea's Stamford Bridge is in the Fulham district. In the ancient past, when football was quite affordable, it was common for fans to attend Fulham games one week and Chelsea the next week, and it remained that way into the 1960s (Chelsea has always been the most successful club in the area). That being said, perhaps a rivalry needs a lot more than geographic proximity. In Catalunya, it is anti- versus pro-independence; in Glasgow, it's Catholics versus Protestants.

It has to be something bigger than geography. A famous player leaving for the rivals, for instance. As for Fulham versus Chelsea, they were in the same division only five times between 1968 and 2001, and the derby has taken place 75 times (the north London derby, for instance, has been contested 200 times).

It is not unusual for Chelsea fans to refer to their neighbours as 'tinpot Fulham'. It is very clear that Fulham fans hate Chelsea more than all, but this delusion of grandeur won't automatically converge into a non-existent rivalry. Fulham supporters have always had a 'not like us' mentality towards Chelsea, which in part explains the historical lack of hooliganism in the Fulham fan base (the Chelsea Headhunters used to be one of the most infamous hooligan firms in English football with a reputation for racism). 'Long-standing Fulham supporters tend to define themselves against what they perceive as the "hooligans" and "glory hunters" at Stamford Bridge. They present a self-image of being more authentic and good-tempered than their rivals,' writes Ramón Spaaij, in his research *Understanding Football Hooliganism*.

The Fulham fan base has been perceived over the years as very friendly. They even used to host a 'neutral section' in the stadium. I read this joke on the Internet once:

> *– What would a Fulham fan do if Chelsea fans invaded their section?*
>
> *– Serve biscuits and a cup of tea!*

Fulham supporters hate Chelsea because of what they represent: an under-achiever that won trophies due to foreign money. There is just a little problem with that perception though. A) Fulham is an under-achiever *that failed* to win trophies with foreign money. B) Chelsea was always better and bigger even when they were poor. Fulham's only victory against Chelsea in the Premier League was in 2006 (Liam was right about it), their first win over Chelsea since 1979. Home fans invaded the pitch to celebrate resulting in a (minor) pitch battle – they didn't serve biscuits and a cup of tea, after all! At the end of the season, however, Mourinho's Chelsea became champions for the second consecutive season.

The Chancellors is a typical supporters' pub with scarves, Fulham photos and newspaper articles on the wall. What caught my attention, though, was a framed Division One standings for the 1950/51 season, with Chelsea at rock bottom. It would've been a great taunt before I discovered it was an unfinished season table: Chelsea ended up winning their last four games, escaping relegation on goal difference. *Fake news!* Not only that: Fulham was the team relegated in the following season instead. I actually felt sorry for the whole dang story.

However, Fulham fans are accustomed to not having big trophies or high-profile players. It is Craven Cottage, the apple of their eyes. It is the symbol of their lingering past as a working-class community that survived in an affluent area of London. The stadium may be the most important thing about Fulham, a ground that is recognisable around the world. Its main stand and corner pavilion are both protected buildings, while the Cottage's exterior brick façade (featuring Fulham's crest) is recognised as a historical heritage building. And, yes, the stadium has a cottage in it, which sits in the corner, converted into a VIP area with expensive seating.

Craven Cottage swims against the tide of the new big stadiums in London. West Ham left their traditional Boleyn Ground, where they played for a century, to take over the (white elephant) Olympic Stadium; Tottenham refurbished White Hart Lane (first opened in 1898) into an arena with the intention to sell the naming rights (and a larger capacity of 61,000); Chelsea recently got permission from London City Hall to renovate Stamford Bridge to increase its capacity from 41,000 to 60,000, starting in the year 2022. Fancy stadiums with cheese rooms and craft beer brewed onsite. Not there. Its Johnny Haynes Stand dates back to 1905 with its original wooden seats. Every pavilion at Craven Cottage has a partially obstructed view, as anti-modern football as you can get, and as nostalgic and uncomfortable as you can imagine. I watched the match in the Hammersmith Stand behind the goal, where the most vocal Fulham fans are concentrated, a few metres from the pitch.

Craven Cottage is neither hostile nor particularly loud, according to several other London fan bases' shared knowledge. Contrary to the intimidating atmosphere at The Den, visiting fans don't feel especially threatened there. It has been said that visiting hooligans in the past wouldn't even turn up at Fulham because they knew there would be no one to fight. Up until recently, Craven Cottage had a designated neutral section if one wanted just to watch a football game (which is now forbidden by the Premier League). Fulham was the last team to have standing accommodation in the Premier League, until the 2001/02 season (also forbidden since then, because, well, they will forbid everything that may result in a little fun).

Of course Fulham fans are nice, but their niceness is exaggerated – they are not the Teletubbies. They curse at the referee and loudly support their players. It was just not as loud as the visiting fans of Leeds United, arguably one of the noisiest crowds in England. Fulham has a visible older and whiter fan base if compared with other London fan bases (I honestly didn't see a single black man or woman in the stadium). Besides their next-door neighbours Chelsea, Fulham is also geographically close to Queens Park Rangers (4.5km) and Brentford FC (6km), but neither fan base has a particular fierce rivalry against Fulham (it is a tendency in football to hate who is above, not below, and that is the reason Fulham fans also don't consider 'tinpot Brentford' to be fierce rivals). There are only two certainties in the west London area: everyone hates Chelsea and nobody hates Fulham.

Like many other clubs in London, the fan base has changed because the area has changed. 'The club's new supporters include a variety of foreign nationals and tourists who seem to be principally attracted by the team's Premiership status. In recent years, the club has also attracted an increasing number of "upper-middle-class" supporters, most of them local residents,' Ramón Spaaij writes in his book. Craven Cottage is a compact stadium that'd be practically perfect for intimidation, but it never quite feels that way.

The loudest night at the stadium, recounted by several supporters, was when Fulham beat Juventus 4-1 in the 2009/10 Europa League quarter-final, one of the most unlikely comebacks in European football history. Fulham lost the first leg 3-1 playing away in Turin, and gave away a goal within two minutes of the second leg, before eventually turning things around. It is a mythical moment for the fans. 'Clint Dempsey's chip [over Buffon] was without a doubt the best moment of my Fulham-supporting career,' Crawford says. The fans had a chant to honour him. 'He scores with his left, he scores with his right, that boy Clint Dempsey, makes Drogba look shite.' It is not every team that can brag about an American footballer being a legend.

Fulham ended up reaching the final, where they lost to Atlético Madrid after extra time. If one asks any supporter, reaching that European final was probably the club's greatest achievement on the pitch. 'If I'd have told people that the team that was at the wrong end of Division Three in the 1990s would be beating Juventus and heading to a European final, they would have thought I was mad!' Crawford says. The singer Lily Allen became viral after the loss as she was filmed breaking down in tears at the stadium (since then she got married to a Chelsea fan, and is considered a traitor by Fulham fans for 'switching loyalties' to their arch-rivals). Remember, eh, you can change your husband and religion, but never your football team.

Fulham has always failed at the final hurdle to win a trophy nonetheless. On top of losing the Europa League Final in 2010, they lost their only FA Cup Final appearance to West Ham in 1975 (when Bobby Moore ironically played for Fulham, making his last appearance at Wembley). Fulham actually won a European trophy in 2002, the UEFA Intertoto Cup, an extinct summer tournament for clubs that had not qualified for the major European competitions (or in some other terms, the 'UEFA Losers League'). The fans have a chant for the achievement in the most cynically *Fulhamish* way: 'We've won it one time, The Intertoto. We've won it one time.'

This fatalism also surrounded Fulham's most iconic player, Johnny Haynes, who spent 18 years playing for the club, with an appearance record of 658 games, and a tally of 158 goals. He was England's captain in the 1962 World Cup, but after a car accident where he severely injured his feet and knee, he was not selected for England's winning squad in 1966. Haynes has his own statue in front of the stadium, and one may conclude that he was clearly more significant to the club's history than Michael Jackson ever was, right?

Johnny Haynes was once described by Pelé as the 'best passer of the ball I've ever seen'.[18] Fulham supporters, by the way, will willingly let one know that Pelé, in fact, scored a goal at Craven Cottage once, when Fulham magically beat Santos 2-1 in March 1973, during a friendly match. Pelé was a three-time World Cup winner at the time, and Santos a powerhouse in the football world; Fulham was just a mid-table second division team. Dan Crawford, the charismatic and diehard Fulham fan, who was born with cerebral palsy, told me much later in the evening that he once interviewed Pelé, after winning a journalism award at the age of 12.

My guess is that Fulham fans will tell such peculiar stories so they can brag about the club's scarce achievements on the pitch. Pelé losing a game to Fulham led us to discuss the movie *Escape to Victory*, starring the Brazilian legend,

---

18 According to Fulham's website. I was never able to find the original quote.

Bobby Moore (and Sylvester Stallone!), when they all defeated the Nazis in a football game! Which led us to talk about Bobby Moore's tenure at Fulham, even if he was past his prime as the English captain in 1966. And then other iconic footballers who played for Fulham, like Sir Bobby Robson (mostly in the second division), and 'the best footballer of all time', George Best, when he was already battling alcoholism.

This Fulham ideology of fatalism and to carry on with their support is an underestimated quality – it is just easy to support a team who win titles every season. Dan Crawford travelled to Brazil for the 2014 World Cup to see all three England matches (in Manaus, São Paulo and Belo Horizonte, 7,190km (4,468 miles) of travelling for the team, and by consequence, the English fan base). As we know, England were eliminated in the group stage without a single win. 'At least we're more used to such failures,' Crawford jokes. The perks of supporting a small team.

When I asked him what is the motivation to support a team who always seems to fail, he gave me this common answer shared by many other fan bases in this journey: 'I am happy to support a club like Fulham, and not, let's say, [Manchester] United or Chelsea, because every victory matters,' he says. 'We'll have a great story to share for a long time. Of course, we have our expectations and dreams, and we'd like to win a big trophy and we've been very, very close to winning it. But somehow Fulham has always found a way to disappoint us all.'

A cold Tuesday night, boosted by the support of 23,000 fans at a packed Craven Cottage, was one of those few memorable moments. Leeds United opened the scoring very early in the game, and Fulham only managed to score an equaliser in the 95th minute to send the stadium into an eruption. Tom Cairney shot a 20-yard cannon, as the ball landed in the net strategically a couple of metres in front of us. After 90 minutes of torture and near defeat, came the excitement as if Fulham had just won their own World Cup. How can you not feel that way after a goal is scored in the 95th minute of a game? It was absolutely chaotic and brilliant.

At the end of the season, Fulham reached the promotion play-offs to the Premier League, and as it happened they fell short by losing to Reading after two legs (four months earlier they beat the exact same opponent 5-0 at the Cottage). Fulham would have to spend one more season playing in the second division. Well, supporting Fulham really is like being on a roller coaster.

Next stop: East London, England
Distance: 25km (16 miles) from Hammersmith
How to get there: 56 minutes on the Tube
The best advice: The Tube system is the best way to navigate the city. Each station has an unmistakable sign with a red circle with a blue bar ... that does not say 'Tube' on it
Soundtrack: 'Don't Stop 'Til You Get Enough' by Michael Jackson

CHAPTER 9

THERE'S NO FOOTBALL
WITHOUT ORIENT

Leyton Orient 0-3 Grimsby Town
Brisbane Road Stadium
Saturday, 11 March 2017
Football League Two (Fourth Division)
Attendance: 5,288

25 May 2014

Wembley Stadium, London. In front of 43,401 fans, Leyton
Orient lost out on promotion to the Championship after
losing to Rotherham United on penalties. The team led 2-0
at half-time before conceding two goals (to a former Leyton
Orient striker, Alex Revell, of all people). However, things
got worse in the shoot-out, when Leyton Orient were 3-2
ahead before missing their last two penalties. They lost 3-4
on penalty kicks. The Orient have been waiting 32 years to
get back to the second tier of English football.

'Everything leading up to the match that day was perfect
and the first half seemed better than perfect,' says Luke Moss,
24, who works at the club's store. 'Then it all came crashing

down. One memory I won't take away from that day is after the final penalty kick in the shoot-out, just looking down and seeing [our midfielder] Romain Vincelot on his knees punching the turf, and some other players in tears.'

22 April 2017

Gresty Road, Crewe. In front of 3,745 fans, Leyton Orient were relegated to the fifth tier of English football following a 3-0 loss away to Crewe Alexandra, 240km (150 miles) from London. Leyton Orient finished the 2016/17 fourth division season dead last and ended their 122 years of history in the Football League. Leyton Orient were on the verge of extinction.

'People ask me who I'd support if Orient were no more. The simple answer is that my interest and love for football would cease to exist if the worst was to happen to my club,' says Luke. 'There are strong indications of a takeover [of the club], and if that were to happen then what we need is stability and to rebuild before we can get back into the Football League.'

Dreams turned into a nightmare for Leyton Orient in less than three years. There is a popular saying in Brazil that says, 'when in Hell, embrace the Devil'. After losing the promotion play-offs to the Championship three years before, the club was sold to Italian Francesco Becchetti, who made his fortune in the waste disposal and recycling business. The new owner's promises when he took over the club were exciting; his experience managing a football club was, well, zero.

East London's Leyton Orient is the second-oldest club in London, and probably the smallest of all to spend at least one season in the top flight of England. In the London hierarchy of football, if we consider titles and fan bases, Arsenal, Chelsea and Tottenham are clearly on top, with West Ham behind them. A second group is made up of Charlton, Queens Park Rangers, Crystal Palace and Fulham, all incredibly close. Wimbledon and Brentford come next in the top ten, and Millwall, even having spent only two seasons in the first division, have a fan base arguably bigger than Leyton Orient. The O's are the nice little one, everybody's second-favourite team.

If everything worked out as originally planned, I would've seen games from four different divisions in London (with the exception of the Premier League, because, who cares). The idea was to cover all geographic areas, watching a football match in the east (Leyton Orient), west (Fulham) and south (Millwall), and finish up north at Barnet FC, which unfortunately I had to skip due to conflicting schedules. Then I visited their Hive Stadium instead, and while they don't technically do tours, you can wander around on your own to take pictures and all. Barnet FC, founded in 1888, have never played a division higher than the fourth tier in English football. It's the only club in London that Leyton Orient has head-to-head advantage over.

When small clubs like Leyton Orient are relegated to the semi-professional leagues in the English pyramid system, it is not only about their dignity and pride. It has practical financial implications, since they cannot be part of the League Cup – losing an opportunity of a cash influx when they advance and get to face a big club. It is harder to come back from the non-leagues as well: only two teams are promoted every season (instead of three) and four clubs are relegated to the amateur leagues (instead of three). The average budget and attendance are lower. It is a snowball effect, and many clubs are never able to recover.

Mat Roper is fiercely loyal to the O's, as he described himself. He has been a Leyton Orient fan since 1978, and he's part of the Leyton Orient Fans' Trust (LOFT). 'You've got to understand that we have had several heartbreaking moments supporting this club, but that is all part of football,' he says. 'Now we needed to put into perspective that our beloved club may be on the brink of losing its existence in a few months, and this is what really breaks our hearts.' His father supported Orient just like his grandfather before him. Roper was holding a donations bucket in front of the stadium together with his teenage son, a fourth-generation Leyton Orient fan.

In March 2017, when I visited the club, they were not only fighting relegation, but their own liquidation. Francesco Becchetti, 51, bought Leyton Orient in 2014 from the boxing promoter kingpin Barry Hearn, who resigned as owner after 19 years. I'm no expert, but managing a football club is not exactly the same as managing a waste disposal company, and the Italian businessman failed. According to journalist (and Orient fan) Tom Davies, 'Becchetti's two-and-a-half-year reign has featured one expensively funded relegation, an unsuccessful Italian reality TV show, a money-laundering investigation, a six-match ban for kicking his then assistant manager, ten head coaches and a chaotic player-recruitment policy,' he wrote in *The Guardian*.

It is highly unusual for small teams to make the news in daily newspapers, but Becchetti put Leyton Orient on

Espanyol supporters in front of the club's bus before the match at Santiago Bernabéu

Rayo Vallecano fans protest in front of the team's locker room at Vallecas stadium

'Love Rayo Hate Racism', the anti-racist mural at Vallecas depicting former Rayo Vallecano footballer Laurie Cunningham

The Allianz Arena exterior is coloured blue for the occasion of TSV 1860 Munich home games

Union Berlin fans hold up scarves prior to the match at Stadion An der Alten Försterei

The sculpture celebrating Union Berlin supporters who worked in the renovation of the club's stadium

St. Pauli supporters at Millerntor-Stadion and their traditional pirate flags

St. Pauli 'regular' supporters at the Nordkurve, the opposite side to the ultras

Strip clubs and casual businesses are side by side in St. Pauli's Reeperbahn Street

A minivan manufactured in East Germany, this Barkas is used to sell Union Berlin merchandise

The 'wall' at The Den stadium celebrating the Millwall supporters

Mounted policemen in front of the Millwall Café opposite The Den

The traditional old wooden seats in the stand at Craven Cottage, London's oldest stadium and home of Fulham FC

A banner at Brisbane Road celebrating Leyton Orient's Division 3 title. Glorious times!

The 51,800-seat Hampden Park opened to 700 Queen's Park FC fans in a Scottish third division match against Livingston

Queen's Park's history-makers, including Ross Caven, who holds the record for the greatest number of appearances at 594; and Eddie Hunter who spent 36 years with the club

The solitary Belenenses scarf at the Estadio da Luz prior to the match against Benfica

CF Belenenses' trophies are displayed at the museum of the Restelo stadium

The weird-looking shaped building behind Red Star's Stade Bauer

The not-so-amicable HQ pub for Red Star fans in front of the team's stadium

The semi-abandoned box office at Stade Bauer since the club was hosting games in Beauvais.

The magnificent façade of Het Kasteel (The Castle), Sparta Rotterdam's stadium

The historical Stadio Olimpico in Turin, unfortunately with a running track separating the crowd from the action

A graffiti design by Torino fans at the Stadio Filadelfia construction site: 'The title doesn't cancel your smell. Juve is shit'

the front pages. 'London's second-oldest club are facing oblivion,' read the headline in the sports section of the *Evening Standard* on 2 March 2017. The chairman was not attending games, players and staff were waiting for their monthly wages and Orient fans urged him to walk away and sell. A winding-up petition against Leyton Orient was due in the High Court over £250,000 in unpaid taxes. The LOFT hoped to raise £100,000, which would help them to join a consortium to buy out Becchetti, a desperate attempt to save the club. 'This is a small club, but it still needs a lot of money to run it,' Roper says. 'It isn't simple, although with our club's extinction being a real possibility, maybe that would be our only way to save Orient from the circus that Becchetti put us in. There is no football without the O's.'

There are successful cases of fan-managed clubs in England, such as Portsmouth, Wycombe Wanderers and Exeter City. They all went down to the fourth division before being taken over by their own supporters' trusts. Unfortunately, they are exceptions. The model most frequently adopted by English clubs is the businessman fetish: a billionaire taking control of the club and leading it to immediate success. They show up with money, convincing words and provocative statements about winning titles. However, there are not too many successful cases to make a case for this type of model. Manchester City and Chelsea are likely the only ones to be considered successful examples (and perhaps Fulham FC, if we ignore the lack of trophies).

Unsuccessful cases, on the contrary, have piled up, and Leyton Orient are not alone when it comes to disastrous leadership. Charlton, Nottingham Forest, Leeds, Morecambe, Coventry and Blackpool are all examples of how a bad administration can single-handedly destroy a traditional football club. Blackpool and Leyton Orient fans even came together to take part in a joint protest in 2016. Blackpool fans were currently boycotting their home games and continued to do so by not going to Wembley for the club's promotion play-off match to the third division.

For these fans, their hate of modern football is not only about some kind of nostalgia for the game. They have been directly affected by the lack of regulations. It is nonsensical to associate businessmen and money with football experience (and passion, which is even more important for the fans). It wouldn't be advised to ask for a brake fluid change by the CEO of General Motors, right? It is not his expertise, if I had to guess. So why are we continuously doing this in football? It is in nobody's interest to hold nouveau riche owners accountable, especially when it's not a so-called big club going downhill. 'Football supporters have been taken for granted for too long by those that own, manage and even write about football clubs,' Tom Davies writes. 'There's an enormous amount of enthusiasm, intelligence and dedication on the terraces that should be better utilized by the club. Fans deserve more of a say in the way the game is run.'

Even though I support a 'big club' myself, I cannot see how it's good for the game in the long run to treat clubs like Leyton Orient as collateral damage (as Darwinist as it sounds). The club's near extinction is not exclusively linked to a shady chairman, but everything in place that allows shady chairmen to keep taking over. Small clubs are kind of an acceptable loss for the 'greater good' of this glorified era of 'professional football'. However, it's hard to imagine regulations not changing if that happened to a club like Liverpool or Manchester United (and their American owners). I know it may sound dramatic, but think about, for five minutes, if it was *your club* that vanished from Earth. We cannot forget what Orient fan Luke said earlier in this chapter: 'People ask me who I'd support if Orient were no more. The simple answer is that my interest and love for football would cease to exist if the worst was to happen to my club.' The game of football is great, but what really brings people together is their clubs.

Leyton Orient have been through a lot of changes throughout their history, which perhaps made it easier for fans to accept an owner not involved in the community. They were founded as Clapton Orient and changed their name to Leyton only after World War II (and further reverted back to simply Orient in 1966, and finally back to Leyton Orient in 1989). The club was based in Hackney until moving further east to its present home at Brisbane Road. Leyton Orient even played in blue colours once, before reinstating the traditional red jersey in the late 1960s (their only appearance in the English first division was, ironically, playing in blue).

However, this time around is different because this change interferes with the club's existence, and apparently nobody even seems to care much about it. 'There is almost zero regard for football supporters anymore, and I'm continuously losing interest and love for English football,' says Luke. 'Ultimately there's just too much money in the game now. Even in non-league football you see clubs spending beyond their means. Ticket prices are a really big issue. If I want to bring a friend to watch Leyton Orient with me, I can't justify them having to spend £25. It's even crazier when you look at bigger clubs charging £60 for an average ticket.'

London was easily the city where I spent the most money on football tickets, even if I have only watched games in lower divisions. I spent more money on tickets than for my seven days of accommodation at a Camden Town hostel. It was undoubtedly expensive to the point that I was budgeting for lunch and dinner, eating Big Macs. To watch football games, I had to give up on other things, such as quality meals and comfortable beds, but I'm just a tourist there, with a disposable income to travel. The fans don't have that luxury when they live in the city.

Especially in London, there is a very high cost of living compared with other cities in Europe. When one stays at a hostel, one will almost certainly come across people actually permanently living there, like my room-mate, who was unemployed. One day I stumbled into a guy breakdancing in front of a Tube station in exchange for tips. The next day, he was there performing magic. He was not living a very glamorous life, I'd assume. However, if I had to guess, he would probably say the same thing about someone travelling abroad and spending their Saturday sunny afternoon watching a mediocre fourth division game.

This little story is not a complete digression, as I think football in England (but especially in London) has come to represent gentrification itself. The bigger clubs offer comfortable stadiums, fancy drinks and superstar players, ultimately forcing the little ones to abide. They offer an experience to their *customers*, which is inherently designed for tourists. But unlike them, Leyton Orient cannot offer success and glamour, and their fans need to be persuaded differently. 'Leyton Orient was my local club, and I didn't start going regularly until I was 14 because they used to give free tickets to my school,' Luke Moss says. 'I went with some friends from school, and I could walk from my house to the stadium in five minutes! I remember being part of their community team, but I wasn't quite talented enough to make it professionally.'

He is an example of where community service worked in the club's favour, although that is not normally the case in the region. Leyton Orient got lucky because Luke's parents weren't too into football, otherwise they'd probably support West Ham and Arsenal, the most popular teams in these parts. Arsenal's stadium is only 10km away from Brisbane Road, and West Ham's stadium, which was already close, moved closer to Leyton Orient's door, to the Olympic Stadium (it's actually possible to see the stadium from Leyton). 'They need more people to fill up their big stadium now, and it is difficult for us to compete,' Jim Marchant says. 'But I love this team more than anything and we will survive.'

Marchant looks like Hollywood's version of a Hell's Angel, with his bushy grey beard, long hair tied with a bandana, and wearing aviator sunglasses and a dirty leather jacket. He has been supporting Leyton Orient for 38 years, he says. 'We have always been a small club throughout our history, and to be honest we're seen as London's second-favourite team. No one has a negative word to say about Leyton Orient.' There is no rivalry between West Ham and Leyton Orient fan bases (mainly because Orient fans are not exactly a threat and were never attached to hooliganism), so the Hammers' relocation had a tremendous impact on Leyton Orient. For a team with an average attendance of 5,000 fans per game, its numbers dwindled, much like a corner store would suffer if a Tesco opened across the street.

According to the English Football League regulation, published on its website, 'any stadium relocation shall abide by certain criteria, such as would not adversely affect Clubs having their registered grounds in the immediate vicinity of the proposed location', a regulation that the EFL chose to solemnly ignore so the Olympic Games 'legacy' would not become a white elephant in the city (as they normally do). Leyton Orient itself pleaded tenancy for the Olympic Stadium, which honestly would make no sense since they cannot sell out their own smaller ground.

While ten more fans don't make such a difference for Arsenal, ten fewer fans have a tremendous impact on Leyton Orient. When a ticket holder is a no-show at Arsenal's Emirates Stadium, the club will resell his ticket instantly – probably to a Singaporean tourist – but a no-show at Brisbane Road likely means an empty seat. When a team doesn't count on its success, they normally appeal to the community, which is difficult with so many big neighbours around. David Beckham was born in Leyton and had trials for his local club Leyton Orient before he left; Iron Maiden's Steve Harris was born in Leyton, and never considered supporting another team in the region other than West Ham. Blur's Damon Albarn supports Chelsea. The competition is brutal.

East London is not exactly a hub for tourists in the city (unless you take into account the hipsters who took over

Hackney, Shoreditch and Dalston), and has historically been one of the poorest areas of London. The Central Line is probably the busiest in the Tube (subway) system, and Leyton is possibly the most diverse part of the borough, a melting pot of different nationalities. It's palpable as soon as you leave the station, where kebab houses, grocery stores, fruit markets, barber shops and everything else are named after Leyton. The food is cheaper there (and better than a Big Mac, obviously), and tourists wandering around are few and far between, even on matchdays. One might argue that Leyton Orient is the proudest London club about their locality: the fan base chants about east London, and the club's social media channels promote being from east London, just to name two examples.

When you reach the Coronation Gardens, closer to the stadium, Leyton is a more predominantly residential area. Laurie Cunningham, the first black man to play for the English team, would have a statue unveiled there later in 2017 – he is the biggest (and perhaps only) superstar to have ever played for Leyton Orient, where he began his career. 'Leyton Orient, a small, close-knit club, offered a welcome that its bigger, more famous neighbour West Ham did not – whose core support was drawn primarily from white working-class dock workers,' according to Cunningham's biography.[19] As I mentioned in Chapter 2, the Leyton Orient prodigy was also the inspiration for the banner 'Love Rayo, Hate Racism' at Vallecas stadium, in Madrid, where he finished his career before his fatal car accident.

---

19 Kavanagh, D., *Different Class: The Story of Laurie Cunningham* (London: Unbound, 2017)

In front of the Brisbane Road stadium, there is a recreational football pitch where I spent half an hour watching an amateur game (at that point I had no way of knowing that the quality of the 'main event' wouldn't be much different to be honest). After buying my ticket for £25, I went to the Supporters' Club bar, beside the box office, where I was probably the youngest patron (I was born in 1980). They specialise in draught beer, including the award-winning Mighty Oak's Oscar Wilde, once named the best in the country (I am not a beer snob; I just thought it would be cool to name-drop this info). The bar is covered in Orient posters, newspapers and memorabilia, mostly from over 50 years ago when they were experiencing their glory.

Leyton Orient played only once in the English first division, when they were promoted in the 1961/62 season alongside Bill Shankly's Liverpool (that would make a great trivia question). Sixty years and 12 national league titles won later, Liverpool are still in the first tier. On the other hand, Orient's first spell in the top division turned out to be a disaster, being relegated immediately back to the second division alongside Manchester City (another good trivia question). Football really changed, especially for Man City, but not so much for Leyton Orient, which doesn't mean their fans didn't enjoy their only season in the 'promised land'.

The club has only two professional titles, highly praised in the banners behind the goal, which I made a point of noting: the 1955/56 Third Division title, and the 1969/70 Third Division title. Another two banners referenced 'The Road to the Promised Land' (citing their promotion to the first division in the 1960s), and 'The 15 Seconds to Glory', when Leyton Orient scored a go-ahead goal against Oxford with only 15 seconds left to play that guaranteed their promotion to League One in the 2005/06 season (their first automatic promotion in 36 years!). Anyway, no one that I spoke with acknowledged this feat as the '15 seconds to glory'.[20]

They came close to a second top-flight spell during Cunningham's tenure as a player. In the 1973/74 season, Leyton Orient just needed to win their last game at home against Aston Villa to guarantee promotion. Of course, they did not. At this point, the fans already know what to expect every time they have higher expectations. 'The average Orient supporter is definitely pessimistic,' Luke Moss says. 'We don't expect success; we're not used to success; that's also what makes the club special for us. We don't watch Leyton Orient expecting to win. We go because it's such a community atmosphere where it feels like everybody knows each other.'

It is that circular argument repeated like a mantra by small-club fans. Every victory counts and makes every celebration more special. The Hell's Angel-looking Jim Marchant, who was in front of the stadium like a mascot, chatting to everyone, remembers a game against Arsenal in the FA Cup in 2011. 'Jonathan Téhoué came in, and scored our goal in the last minute to give the stadium a roar sound like no other,' he says. 'Everyone erupted like a volcano; definitely one of the most memorable nights at Brisbane.' Arsenal won 5-0 in the replay.

---

20 The broadcasting commentary is absolutely priceless, though.

The club's success comes always with a bit of failure, like the 2013/14 season that finished on penalty kicks. 'It's my favourite moment supporting the team. With the points tally we had, most other seasons we would have won the league,' Luke Moss says. (Wolverhampton's 103 points that season is a League One record.) 'But to get to the play-off final at Wembley was amazing,' he continues, referencing the game that opened this chapter. Success is going from failure to failure with no loss of enthusiasm, or so an impostor philosopher once said.

Leyton Orient are not just having a spell of bad luck (its more like 100 years of bad luck). In a 1995 low-budget student documentary, *Orient: Club for a Fiver*, the production follows the misfortunes of Leyton Orient during the 1994/95 season, in which they failed to win away from home, and ended the season with nine straight defeats. This film is highly recommended to those interested in real football, such as unrestricted access to the dressing room, no social media releases, unfiltered tantrums. A team with no money falling to pieces.

The film's leading star is head coach John Sitton, with his wild outbursts as he tries to motivate his players. He offers to fight two players in one of his diatribes. 'You can pair up if you like, and you can fucking pick someone else to help you, and you can bring yer fackin' dinner because by the time I'm finished with ya you'll fackin' need it,' he says in his thick accent. Sitton was never able to coach another professional team (today he works as a cab driver in London, constantly complaining about Uber through his Twitter account). Leyton Orient finished that season obviously relegated, and the club was put up for sale for £5 (a fiver), when Barry Hearn became their chairman until he finally sold the club to Becchetti in 2014 for £4m (good margin, eh!).

The documentary deserved an Oscar for Football Failures, but it was not the club's rock bottom. Leyton Orient's rock bottom is now. They were dead last in the fourth division, in need of a miracle in their last ten matches to avoid relegation. The team was the worst that I saw, a bunch of kids in a league with intense physical contact, an intimidating atmosphere and veterans who know how to trash talk and give everyone a hard time. Grimsby Town dominated the game entirely with Leyton Orient players looking like puppies being led around by their owners in the park – Orient played well until they got tired and ultimately gave up. Grimsby Town's playmaker Dominic Vose's performance was somewhat like a Zidane from the lower leagues.

The visiting fans gave a show apart from their winning celebration. As we know, away games are a huge tradition in English football, only comparable to Germany (not like in France, Italy and Portugal, and most definitely not like in Spain). Nick Hornby once wrote in *Fever Pitch*, his autobiographical story detailing his support for Arsenal, that he learned more about the country in away games than at high school. Grimsby is 300km (186 miles) away from London and the club holds the attendance record for a non-league match, when they won a National League promotion once against Bristol Rovers in front of a 47,029 crowd at Wembley Stadium. The club spent six years outside the Football League (where Leyton Orient was about to be relegated from). 'It feels like the end of the world, but then you get used to it,' says Thomas, who made the three-hour trip to London. 'The team keeps playing and then you keep coming. What else can you do, eh mate? We were there when we played Chelsea [in the FA Cup in 1996], and we were there when we played fuckin' Lincoln City [in the Conference League]. It is about our football club, not the league we play.' Ironically enough, Leyton Orient's '15 Seconds to Glory', when they got promotion in the 2005/06 season, was precisely at the expense of Grimsby Town's fall. Sometimes football is astonishingly cruel.

The Brisbane Road stadium has a capacity of 9,000 and is reminiscent of a community fair in the countryside, with a zinc-roofed pavilion where the club's name is engraved. The washrooms reminded me of those one will find at a bus station in ghost towns. The crowd is pretty much on top of the players and I watched the game from behind the goal, in the Tommy Johnston South Stand, generally where the most noise is made. Johnston is Leyton Orient's all-time leading scorer with 123 goals to his name, in two spells playing for the O's in the late 1950s and early 1960s (his ashes are interred there in the stands named in his honour).

The crowd seemed to run out of patience, cussing and harassing with anger. Everyone but their own players; on the contrary, the fans recognised their effort even if it turned out to be useless. Their fury was against Becchetti and Becchetti only (fans wearing shirts that lampooned his face with a clown nose). 'He's running this club like a complete circus,' they said. The atmosphere in the stadium was completely abnormal due to the club's situation, but from time to time the fans would start singing 'Stand up for the Orient', and other chants.

In the last ten matches of the season, Leyton Orient lost eight, and they were relegated out of the Football League for the first time in the club's history. In the last home game of the season against Colchester, the fans invaded the pitch in protest and the referee had to stop the match (the game was later concluded behind closed doors). 'Fans are the lifeblood of any club, and with ever-growing problems in the game, I want a Leyton Orient for future family generations to support,' Mat Roper says, of the Leyton Orient Fans' Trust. Ironically enough, the league was won by Portsmouth FC, which has recently become a fan-owned football club, following their relegation to the fourth division after being taken over by a Saudi businessman.

It all comes down to different expectations in football. Arsenal fans were massively campaigning for 'Wenger Out' during those times, and three months later their team won the FA Cup Final. In Leyton Orient's small world, where 'globalisation' and 'modern football' will come in the form of a semi-professional league, winning a title at Wembley would not be something to protest. Not now or in 100 years. 'It would be my dream to see Orient win the FA Cup at Wembley, but I'd also settle for us being a solid Championship side,' Luke Moss says, who left his part-time job with the club to work for a media and resourcing company. 'Working on matchdays gave me a good insight into how hard the staff at the club work. It's difficult to say what's ahead at the moment. If Becchetti remains in control of the club then we have no future.'

Francesco Becchetti sold Leyton Orient to Dunkin' Donuts CEO Nigel Travis in July 2017, and therefore the club was saved from liquidation. Apparently, the O's are his childhood team, and from now on, I will truly hope that all Leyton Orient fans have a sweeter life. That being said, with everything positive about football globalisation, such as better infrastructure, comfortable seats, and that floors not completely covered in piss, the most damaging effect was the naturalisation of football fans seen as customers. The fan bases of the super-rich clubs, especially, are more and more impatient every season, accepting nothing but winning it all. *This is what they pay for*, after all. Except that no customer will ever raise £100,000 through donation buckets in front of their favourite store to avoid its bankruptcy; they are customers precisely because they will go with whatever deal is better for them.

Instead of seeing Leyton Orient play in League Two, I could've gone to the Emirates where Arsenal were playing in the Premier League. The next day, Tottenham played at White Hart Lane and a day after, Chelsea took on Manchester United at Stamford Bridge. It was a marvellous weekend for the football clientele. At Brisbane Road, though, the fans are more than patrons.

Next stop: Lisbon, Portugal
Distance: 1,585km (985 miles)
How to get there: Two hours and 40 minutes by plane
The best advice: Try to learn some Portuguese, even if you speak (Brazilian) Portuguese
Soundtrack: 'Strange Town' by The Jam

CHAPTER 10

THERE IS ONLY ONE BELENENSES

Benfica 4-0 Belenenses
Estádio da Luz
Monday, 14 March 2017
Primeira Liga (First Division)
Attendance: 53,897

Sympathetic *(adjective)*
showing that you approve of someone or something or that
you share their views and are willing to support them

- *to be sympathetic to Belenenses supporters*
- *football fans are largely sympathetic to Belenenses*

An incredible number of fans I spoke with in Lisbon
describe Belenenses as sympathetic. They are the easy-to-
like team in the Portuguese capital, frequently patted on the
head as everyone's second-favourite team. However, when
one reads between the lines, the compliment may imply
a negative connotation. Remember at high school about
asking the pretty girl what she thought about you and then
she said you were *adorable*?

Well, it's a bit like that with Belenenses.

Football fans, normally, don't want anybody's admiration. They don't want to feel like their teams are harmless, and many don't see 'sympathetic' as a quality. Rui Vasco Silva, 39, ticket holder No. 7,795 (as he made a point of saying), is one of those fans. 'Whether it is true that Belenenses won't win many games against the richest teams these days, it is also true that we have a history of victories against them, something that cannot, and should not, be ignored,' he says. 'I don't know if we are sympathetic or friendly. What I do know is that we want to be unapologetic and winners.' It is an interesting point: teams winning titles, season after season, are rarely seen as friendly, or sympathetic. Usually everyone hates them.

In Portugal, three teams definitely don't need any sympathy. Benfica, Porto and Sporting have dominated the league, winning every championship since 1935 except for two seasons (and Sporting themselves last won the league in 2001/02). The Big Three have supporters from all over the country, and with the exception of two teams locally supported in the northern cities of Braga (pop. 192,000) and Guimarães (pop. 158,000), anywhere you go in Portugal it will be easy to find either a Benfica, Porto or Sporting fan. The Belenenses fans refer to them as 'eucalyptus' for sucking everything around them away. 'Football culture these days is totally based on results, so people are more interested around an idea of victory than a passion or identity,' Rui Vasco says. 'Why would a person born and raised in Viseu [328km (204 miles) from Lisbon] support Benfica instead of their local club Academico? It confuses me,' he says.

In 2016, a TV interview became viral when a superfan of União de Leiria said before a game against Benfica that he would support ... Benfica! Every country has nationally supported clubs, sure, but Portugal took it to an extreme level, and 90 per cent of fans support the Big Three. As it happens Belenenses fans are on the doorstep of two of them in Lisbon. Like Braga or the Vitoria Guimarães fan base, Belenenses fans don't ever support a 'second club'. José Fidalgo, 41, believes that they're special precisely for that reason. 'We are entrenched between two national clubs and we managed to survive,' he says. 'Whenever I am asked whether I am Benfica or Sporting, I have to explain that our city is not limited to these two possibilities. We will always have a say here in Lisbon and we don't have a second club. We're Belém and Belém only.' Most fans call their club Belém, the region where the club is located.

Success is not what all the supporters in this book can rely on. All these fan bases were mostly born out of family tradition or neighbourhood connections: Belenenses' perseverance is related to both. The club is almost a community association, and they have teams in basketball, handball, futsal and roller hockey (Portugal is a 16-time World Cup champion, whatever that means). Francisco de Carvalho, 23, competes for Belenenses as a triathlete. He has been a fan since he was born, when his father made him a club ticket holder.

'Of course the first reason I became a fan is because of the family tradition; my grandfather, my father, my older brother ... they are all Belenenses and I have been to Restelo [stadium] since I was a kid,' he says. 'The second reason I can't really explain. There are things you feel, *pronto*.'

(Portuguese people have a tendency to finish many sentences with the expression *pronto*, which is a literal translation for 'ready', but contextually means 'that's it').

Rui Vasco has similar connections with family and the district he grew up in. 'From a very early age, I started coming to football games with my maternal grandfather,' he says. 'I heard him tell stories about games at Salésias [stadium] since I was a child, and also about the connection between our club and the city, in particular the western districts like Belém and Ajuda.' Salésias, in the neighbouring district of Ajuda, was the club's stadium until 1956, when they moved to the much bigger Restelo (the old stadium became too small for their fan base, ironically).

Those times of big crowds are now over: Belenenses have a very small fan base. Family-friendly and super niche, their average attendance in the 2016/17 season was 3,800 fans, with a 24 per cent occupancy rate at Restelo (third worst in the league). It is inevitable that compared to Benfica (52,000) and Sporting (40,000), a small club like Belenenses can't compete in popularity with the two giants next door. However, it is also true that the club doesn't even try much.

Belém is a historical place with many outstanding tourist attractions: Belém Tower, Jerónimos Monastery, museums and the birthplace of world famous Portugal egg tarts (Pastel de Belém) – the supporters' nickname is '*pasteis*' because of the pastry. The magnificent official residence of the President of Portugal is located in Belém. It is a beautiful region, on the banks of the Tagus river, right from where those sailor dudes left a long time ago in big caravels, and arrived in Brazil from the Atlantic to claim that they had 'discovered' the land.

Situated on a hill, the Restelo Stadium is only a few minutes' walking distance from all these sites. It has a wonderful view of the river's suspension bridge, and the Christ the King monument (which is probably one of the best views I've seen at a football stadium). It's a visit that totally pays off, whether you are a football fanatic or not. Although, be warned that it is very hard to find the stadium just walking around, if you're not from the city: there are no signs, banners or ads in the area that will lead you to believe there is football nearby. The only thing related to Belenenses I could find was a kiosk on the esplanade supposedly selling the club's merchandise (it was unfortunately closed on Mondays).

When I first visited the Restelo on vacation in 2011, the staff were almost taken aback when they saw me, a tourist, directing me to different entrances and not really knowing where I should sit. Look, I don't need any 'fan service' or special treatment; I'm just a regular football guy. However, these little things matter for a club in need of more revenue. Benfica is a 'eucalyptus' sucking away everything also because they use a national passion to their advantage. They take every opportunity to impress and this has nothing to do with modern football.

It was my second visit to Lisbon and for the second time I deliberately chose to see a Belenenses game. This time, I had to change my whole schedule after the Portuguese league switched dates last minute (it's crazy to deal with the Portuguese league's lack of organisation). All plans adjusted, I had to leave London for Lisbon instead of going directly to Paris, which geographically and financially would make no sense to me. Anyway, 'here I was again on my own'.[21] Technically I could receive a Belenenses Medal of Honour for my effort. Said no one ever.

Six years later, in front of the Estádio do Restelo to buy a ticket, in the early afternoon of a business day, the empty car park seemed like a scene from *The Walking Dead*. Not a single soul was around and I don't know why I'd expect differently. The game was at Benfica's Estádio da Luz, but at Restelo was my only option to buy a ticket for the away section (which I had to figure out through Benfica since Belenenses' press office never answered my email).

In a little room similar to a high school principal's office, an indifferent lady sold me the ticket, before ushering me out of the door, as I craned my neck to see the historical photos on the wall. Then she impulsively asked me whether I was a Vasco da Gama fan (a club from Rio de Janeiro named after one of those sailor dudes in big caravels in the Atlantic), since the two clubs have a similar crest of a red cross of the Order of Christ (*Cruz de Cristo*). 'Nah, I'm Cabral,' I said.[22]

The Portuguese are overall nice and kind, but grumpy at the same time. Taxi drivers complain about everything from the weather to the government. At restaurants, if something is not on the menu, don't even bother asking because, well, it's not on the menu. I naively asked a 60*ish*-year-old ice cream vendor in Belém what he thinks about Belenenses. Bad mistake. 'I don't like football and players make too much money. They don't pay my bills; they don't

---

21 *Goin' down the only road I've ever known.*

22 Pedro Alvares Cabral is the 'discoverer' of Brazil, so I was irrestibly making fun of it.

care about us.' He didn't even have good things to say about Cristiano Ronaldo.

When I visited Belenenses back in 2011, they were in the second division and the attendance was lower (1,735), the average age considerably higher and therefore grumpier. It was a full-on display of bad moods and nagging over a miserable 0-0 score. In Portugal, people choose their words very carefully and don't curse like in the English, Italian or Brazilian stadiums. 'You're not doing anything right, oh poor boy,' a senior shouted to the right-back. 'I think you need a good night's sleep,' shouted another. The cursing was juvenile, but the thing is: in a semi-empty stadium with a 20,000 capacity, the players could definitely hear it. Almost like Fernando Pessoa himself was in the stadium, writing his poetry about how uselessly they performed.

The Restelo location is fantastic, but the stadium has seen better days. Its running track has too big of a gap between the action and the crowd; the walls haven't seen a good coat of paint for several decades; the turnstiles may be the same ones since its 1956 inauguration. The crowd is always small (in 2007, Belenenses played Bayern Munich in the UEFA Cup in front of 7,000). The atmosphere at Restelo is always dull, but also nostalgic – it is an all-seated, oval-shaped stadium so if you're not looking for a gourmet-type arena, it is actually pretty nice.

Although if one is not looking for football nostalgia, I'd recommend the stadiums of the other two Lisbon football clubs. Sporting's Alvalade Stadium is modern and big in an upscale area of the city (the club, who have developed Ronaldo, Luís Figo and eight of the 11 players who started for Portugal in the Euro 2016 Final, have always been the aristocrats in town). When I watched a game there in 2011, the ambience was electric, even though I was surrounded by a sexagenarian fraternity. On that particular vacation, I was only able to make a tour at Estádio da Luz (Stadium of Light), a historical stadium in Europe. This time around I would have a chance to see an actual game, the Lisbon derby of Benfica versus Belenenses.

After I bought my ticket at Restelo, I spent the entire afternoon eating something like 23 types of pastries – I highly recommend going for a *pastel de cerveja* (beer cake) – and talking to people, such as the grumpy ice cream vendor. I had time to kill before meeting up the *Fúria Azul* ultras in front of the Restelo (and to Benfica's stadium from there). Unfortunately, they never showed up with as promised, so I headed to the police station near Estádio da Luz alone, from where allegedly all Belenenses supporters would be escorted to the stadium. Nope, that didn't happen either, despite it being announced on the club's media channels. As frustrated as I was, it made sense to me: an 'escort' to the stadium felt so unnecessary, like winter gloves in the Sahara.

Estádio da Luz is just across from the largest shopping mall in Portugal, and its food court becomes a pre-match meeting point. Fans from all over the country travel to see Benfica on a regular basis, so the stadium is almost like a sanctuary for them. There is a gigantic mural in a tunnel on the way to the stadium, painted with Benfica's eagle symbol, a mandatory stop for family photos and selfies. The surrounding areas are full of vendor kiosks and a red sea of Benfica merchandising, not to mention limitless street food (*bifana* is the highlight in Portugal). A solitary Belenenses blue scarf hung in a kiosk, but I already had mine on my shoulders. I was a convert to the cause. In Portugal, fan bases are called *adeptos*. They are not fans or supporters; they're adepts, so maybe I was an adept to the cause as well.

Upon entering, I was frisked like never before on the entire trip, as if Belenenses *adeptos* were a real threat. There were no more than 100 of us, on the third floor of the stadium (a good location considering I only paid €13), completely separated from Benfica fans. Estádio da Luz is the biggest stadium in Portugal, roof-covered and all-seater for 64,000 fans. However, Belenenses fans are not easily impressed, as they call it Galinheiro da Luz (Chicken Coop of Light, a play on words with the Benfica symbol). Before the kick-off, the sanctuary became a cult: Benfica fans screamed for every player announced, before an eagle flew over the pitch before landing in the club's crest (it was a real eagle! They have two birds trained: Vitória and Gloriosa). This pre-game celebration finished with the whole stadium singing the Benfica anthem. There is no 'You'll Never Walk Alone' here.

The majority of Belenenses fans at the stadium were part of the ultras *Fúria Azul* (Blue Fury), who arrived after all. José Fidalgo, a cosmetic shop owner, was not; instead he was sitting by himself with his 12-year-old daughter. He grew up in Belém (of course he did), and made the decision to not follow his father's path, a Benfica supporter. 'People normally associate with victories, but I don't think it should be like that, and to me it is more important to support my local club,' he says. 'Our support for a football club is borne in each of us more out of conviction than out of will.' That really made me think, as his words had no moral value or sense of pretension. Actually, it sounded almost like a confession. He wants his young daughter to understand why he supports a team who will never win. *It takes more conviction than will.*

Adeptos of Belenenses propel themselves with this type of mentality. Of course they don't want to lose or deliberately support a team that never succeeds (who would?). It only happens that winning is a wide concept, especially in football with only a few trophies in dispute. It takes conviction to not abandon what you love, and football generally ignites the opposite: the shittier the results, the more we support our club. It is definitely not what a person normally does when their favourite TV show starts to tank in quality: people just give up (with the exception of *Star Wars* fans, of course, who continue watching no matter how stupid it has become).

It is just as easy to choose Porto, Benfica or Sporting if one lives in Portugal (or abroad – there is a big Portuguese community in Toronto). From the small clubs' perspectives, there is not only an economic gap, but other hurdles, like the bigger clubs are favoured by the referees. 'There is a continued practice of favouring the three eucalyptuses, which gives them more visibility, more access to financial resources and ultimately more victories,' Rui Vasco says. Being helped by the referees is far from being the sole explanation for the Big Three's monopoly in Portugal, although it is absurdly easy to spot this unfair practice. Benfica and Porto fans evidently disagree: Benfica fans think that only Porto is favoured, and Porto fans think the opposite.

José Fidalgo, despite all his dislike for what the Big Three represent in football, is never anti-Portugal when it comes to the European competitions. A week before Belenenses took on Benfica, the Lisbon giants were eliminated from the UEFA Champions League after losing 4-0 to Borussia Dortmund, and I asked Fidalgo whether he was happy with the result. 'We have to support Portugal because it is good for our morale as a country and it's also good for all the [Portuguese] clubs due to the [UEFA] ranking system,' he argues. Some fans see the situation differently, but there are three things that Portugal agrees on: they have a lot of pride in being Portuguese; they breathe and sweat football; and Cristiano Ronaldo is God.

Benfica and Belenenses is a historical derby in Lisbon, even if there's a big disparity between them. They have faced each other 240 times, and Belém has only won 59 times (or 24.5 per cent).[23] Moreover, Belenenses has never beaten Benfica as a visitor in the new Estádio da Luz, opened in 2003, and it was no surprise when Benfica scored first in the 11th minute, following a defender trying to pass back to the goalkeeper with his chest (everybody knows that trying to pass back to the goalkeeper with your chest is the No. 1 rule of what not to do on the pitch).

Benfica scored their second, third and fourth goals in the second half, while Belenenses had a total of zero shots on target. It was not surprising either, since their best striker, Maurides, was once stretchered off with a knee injury after a somersault goal celebration went wrong while playing for the Brazilian team Internacional (yeah, that's right, my team again). The game finished 4-0, which did not shock the group of Belenenses ultras, who kept chanting. They

---

23 As of February 2021.

don't like to lose, but they're used to it, and their passion for the Cross of Christ speaks louder.

'You're clowns! Go home, you bunch of clowns,' screamed 'dona' Mercedes towards Benfica fans taking selfies on the level below us. Mercedes, 51, has been attending games at Restelo since the 1980s, with her uncles and cousins, because her father supports Benfica. 'My father is the *red sheep* of our family,' she laughs, loudly at her own joke. 'The best day of my life was when we beat Benfica in the cup final.' That was in 1989, over three decades ago. Mercedes was cursing the Benfica fans out because we needed to wait for every Benfica supporter to leave before we could exit the stadium; we're told by the security stewards to wait for them. Even if the game is a local derby, it did not make much sense, either, because just like before the game, any violence there was as likely as rain in the Sahara.

The evening ended business as usual for Benfica fans, who at the end of the season celebrated their record of 36 Portuguese league titles. To celebrate, all the fans gathered in the Marquês do Pombal Square, and I only know this because earlier in the day Fidalgo told me (for no apparent reason) that the Marquis's remains are placed in Belém. Also, he told me that Benfica was actually founded in a pharmacy in Belém. These two pieces of information are correct; I just couldn't understand his enthusiasm for them. He was somehow bragging about them.

Perhaps because Belenenses fans are obsessed with the past, which is the only time they had glory and success, they talk about little achievements as if they were heroic feats, part of Luís de Camões's *The Lusiads*. Belenenses is one of only two clubs outside the Big Three to have ever won the national league, in 1946 (they won three championships in the 1930s during the amateur era, which the fans also consider a national title). There was effectively a 'Big Four' in Portugal at the time, and Belenenses was the team invited to play in the inauguration of Real Madrid's Nuevo Estadio Chamartín (renamed later to Santiago Bernabéu).

Other than Benfica, Porto and Sporting, Belenenses is the club with more appearances in the Portuguese league's top four. On the other hand, in 84 seasons of the Portuguese league, Belenenses is the only club to lose a title in the last round. It was in 1975, when earlier in the season more than 60,000 fans were at Restelo to see Belenenses beat rivals Benfica 4-2 (they ended up finishing third).

'We have a great history, but we should not be clinging to the past only,' José Fidalgo says. 'This also depends on us, because we can't be successful if we don't look ahead, and to the future,' he says, ironically, before talking about legendary goalkeeper Félix Mourinho, who played in Belém from 1968 to 1974. 'In an ironic twist of destiny,' he told me, 'his son José won his first game as head coach for Benfica against Belenenses.' José Mourinho was 37 then (at the age of 19 he also briefly played and scored a couple of goals for Belenenses).

Belenenses' 'Special One', however, is the Brazilian head coach Marinho Peres, who was in charge when they won their last big trophy in the 1989 Portuguese Cup, ending a streak of 29 years. Belenenses beat none other than Benfica in the final. 'He is loved by the fans not only for winning the Portuguese Cup, but he has since returned when the club needed his help,' Rui Vasco says. 'His name is part of our history and the fans will never forget.' Belenenses beat all the Big Three to win the cup, which had never happened before or since then.

In 2012, Belenenses was taken over by Codecity Sports Management, with the idea of running a more 'professional' football club. 'They are totally disconnected from our fan base, our history and our soul,' Rui Vasco says. 'They can't understand and are not willing to understand the people who give their blood to this club. We, as fans, are not a company and they haven't done anything positive for our football either.' It doesn't help that Codecity's CEO, Pedro Soares, while working at Portugal Telecom, facilitated a business that gave the Premier League exclusive broadcasting rights to Benfica TV (yes, a football club owning TV rights).

After the takeover, the Belenenses SAD (the sport limited company) became a new entity, and an internal war between club and the SAD had started. The script is a well-known story in modern football. The investors came, and they made an initial investment big enough for the club to reach the Europa League. The money has dried up since then, the football results flopped and the fans are now discontent with the lack of communication. The ultras have been protesting at home games for years, and attendance has significantly dropped. Football is not business, at least not to supporters willing to spend money to see mediocre football only out of passion.

In June 2018, the inevitable happened, and the club Belenenses announced their independence from the SAD, the administrators, and ceased to have any relationship. The club Belenenses retained the team's achievements, history, the crest and the Restelo Stadium, and claimed there is only one Belenenses. The SAD kept the current professional team (as they hold players' economic rights), the licence to play in the first division, but they had to change their logo (to a questionable tower representing Belém). CF Belenenses became an independent entity and celebrated their 100-year anniversary playing in the sixth division (a Lisbon league). The fans are on their side, and the support for Belenenses SAD became the worst in the league.

The battle ended up as a *fado* song immersed in Portuguese drama. The history of a little guy not wanting his house to be the playground of some buyer in a fancy suit. Even if that meant starting over, playing amateur games in Lisbon. Their enthusiasm when talking about their little club is like no other, and a visit to Restelo is worthwhile. It is unique, and every curse sounded poetic. It is very easy to understand why people feel sympathetic towards Belenenses.

Next stop: Paris, France

Distance: 1,450km (900 miles)

How to get there: Two and a half hours by plane

Best advice: Beauvais is not Paris. It is not even remotely close. Fuck off, Ryanair!

Soundtrack: 'Ça plane pour moi' by Plastic Bertrand

CHAPTER 11

RED STAR PARIS IS A FEAST

Red Star 0-1 Amiens
Stade Jean-Bouin
Friday, 17 March 2017
Ligue 2 (Second Division)
Attendance: 4,093

Red Star FC is a legendary football club in Paris, except that only a few people might know about their existence. They are more historical than Qatar-backed club Paris Saint-Germain, the giants in town. And while Red Star do not have as many titles, an elite status or big crowds like PSG, they have 120 years of football tradition. However, what does tradition really mean in football? I reckon that there is a subtle difference between being a traditional club or a big club, and lately that distinction has become very debatable in football circles, especially in this era of new money. So here's my 15 cents about it.

Tradition, in its literal meaning, is what has existed (or resisted) from generation to generation, or the fact of being passed on this way. But, then, how long is long enough? Bayern Munich, for example, was never a successful team until the 1970s, but it is arguably perceived as a traditional football club these days. They are traditional and big, which is a concept inherently attached to the club's successes on the pitch, which is more subjective (a club may have success in its national league, but not at all on the continent, for instance). Of course, it can go hand in hand for several teams (Barcelona, Juventus, Liverpool, and, I rest my case, Bayern). But, then, how do you measure success? When are you successful enough? Winning seven national leagues, like PSG did recently, but never a UEFA Champions League, is not enough to deserve their badge of honour of 'tradition'? In conclusion, it all depends.

I will play devil's advocate for Paris Saint-Germain here, only for the sake of the argument. The lack of football DNA of PSG, for many people, comes from the fact that it is a very new club (only 50 years old) with the majority of their trophies won within the last decade (after the Qatari money investment). However, what about Manchester City, a 140-year-old club with most of their trophies won in the last decade? Do they lack football DNA or are they old enough to be considered 'traditional'? Had I made this trip in 2010, it would be very obvious to consider Manchester City in the shadow of local giants. So, I guess what I'm saying here is despite the fact that it is aggravating that football clubs became merely toys for billionaire investors to play with, we cannot ignore their results on the pitch. I hate it too, but it is real. And all that being said, I would put it simply like this: PSG is a big club without the tradition; Red Star FC is a traditional club without the money.

Red Star is the second-oldest club in France, for instance, but small in every other aspect. The last time they played first-tier football was in 1975; the club's infrastructure is precarious and they have (probably) the smallest fan base in this book. Tradition is all that Red Star has left. The club was founded by Jules Rimet, FIFA's longest-serving president and the World Cup 'inventor'. Red Star dominated French football in the 1920s winning four French Cups, including a three-peat (in the professional era, they only won a title in 1942). Red Star was a founding member of the French league and became especially popular in the north area of Paris.

The club went bonkers especially after World War II, unluckily being relegated to the second division a year before the French league was suspended for six years. Not that football was what really mattered in the country at that time. Red Star's stadium was literally used as a safe place to store weapons during German occupation. Jean-Claude Bauer, a doctor who the Stade Bauer is named after, was shot by the Nazis in 1942, due to his involvement with the Communist Party – and even if Red Star fans are in fact associated with left-wing movements these days, the club's name has nothing to do with communism (Red Star was founded nearly two decades before the Bolshevik Revolution). Their peculiar English name for a French club is most likely a reference to the Red Star Line, a shipping company linked to Rimet's governess (which is kind of boring, but at least it is not White Star, aka *Titanic*'s manufacturer).

Even if the name is a funny coincidence, Red Star has been indeed labelled as a socialist club. In 2015, France's former president François Hollande paid a visit to Red Star's stadium in Saint-Ouen, where he recalled his frequent trips as a student, and made a statement about Red Star's 'embodiment of a diverse and multicultural France'. Founded in 2004, the Collectif Red Star Bauer embraced Antifa ideology and started bringing flags and banners to the stadium celebrating former player Rino Della Negra. A 19-year-old born in France to Italian parents, he joined the Parisian Resistance and was executed by the Nazis in 1944. 'Say hello and goodbye to all in Red Star,' he wrote in his last letter to his brother. The story was revealed only at the beginning of the 2000s, but a rebel football player is too good an image to let go of, so Collectif Bauer adopted Della Negra as a symbol of the club. Red Star supporters can be considered a low-budget version of St. Pauli: they were lefties before it was a thing.

Unlike St. Pauli, however, their fan base has severely declined since the 1960s. Red Star fans are mostly from the multi-ethnic suburb of Saint-Ouen, in the north of Paris (the *département* with the highest proportion of immigrants in the country), and they would attract larger crowds back then. Club historian Gilles Saillant, 65, told *Vice Magazine*: 'At the time, we could see meetings against Marseille, Saint-Étienne or Nantes. Every big game the stadium was full, with almost 18,000 fans.' Saillant used to live in a building opposite the stadium, and he completed 50 seasons of supporting Red Star in 2018, but was unfortunately unavailable when I was in Paris.

The 1970s proved to be a terrible decade for Red Star, a combination of successive misfortunes. The club was playing in the second division + Paris Saint-Germain was founded + French football faced arguably its lowest era (France did not qualify for the World Cups in 1970 and

1974). At some point Red Star were even relegated to the fourth division, and saw their popularity vanish, mostly becoming a semi-professional club. Perhaps what makes Red Star a traditional club is the simple fact that they still exist.

Paris was never a football town before PSG was blessed by a sheikh's money. It is a city of ten million and has a strong economy, but with a large contingent of migrants from other working-class cities like Marseille and St. Etienne, where their local teams are massively popular. Take it as an example that the only two times that Red Star was able to host a match in the grandiose national stadium, Stade de France were against St. Etienne in front of 45,900 fans in March 1999, and against Olympique de Marseille in front of 51,000 fans in January 2012. Despite the large crowds that turned up to each game, they were supporting, obviously, the visiting teams.

Paris has historically embraced more the France national team than rallied behind their local teams in the league (until recently, even PSG hardly filled half of their stadium). There are socio-economic reasons for it, according to French historian Paul Dietschy in his book,[24] here translated from French:

> For many years football in Paris was seen as something 'to watch', like a spectacle, rather than something to support. In cities like London, Rome or Madrid, the success of football was not based on a social event, but on the fact that it caused people a sense of identity in society.

---

24   Dietschy, P., *Histoire du Football* (Paris: Éditions Perrin, 2010)

Being passionate about football clubs was always something associated with the working class, and Parisians were not keen on being perceived as blue-collar workers.

I might speculate about a second cause for Paris's historical disdain for football. Although the beautiful game remains the number one sport in France, rugby always attracted the elite. The sport is a religion in southern France (Grenoble, Toulon, Toulouse, Bordeaux), with Paris being a sole exception and having traditional clubs in the league. The first-ever rugby league final in France took place in 1892 between two Paris-based teams, Stade Français and Racing Club (teams still up and running after 130 years). Their average attendance is four times lower than PSG these days, although with a historical presence in the city. During a day off, I was walking along the banks of the Seine, near Notre-Dame, thinking about love, life, lust and Camus ('All that I know most surely about morality and obligations, I owe to football,' he once wrote), when suddenly I spotted a Soccer Shop (real name), all covered with PSG flags. Its owner, originally from Biarritz, a city close to the Spanish border, is a big rugby fan. 'Many tourists look for products of Paris Saint-Germain and France, and the store's name is to get their attention. I'm not a huge soccer follower myself,' he says. Well, I could tell. More than 80 per cent of a Soccer Shop in downtown Paris had rugby apparel.

It's pure empiricism, but I believe that the lack of a local team rivalry also contributed to Paris having been historically flat towards football. Local derbies make fan bases elevate their following, to the point that they want to outsize each other (by showing up at stadiums, chanting louder, even buying more jerseys than the rival). Paris never came close to that, especially because PSG is such a young club. They were founded in 1970 after a merger with Paris FC (a club with similar colours and a crest with the Eiffel Tower), restarting from the third division.

Red Star and PSG have faced each other only six times in their history (including PSG's first game ever at Parc des Princes), and only once in the first division. It was a local derby with no fierce rivalry, and it hasn't changed much since. 'We are a very small club compared to them, even if our history is older,' says Thierry, 47, a Gang Green ultras supporter. 'There is no war between us since we don't compete in the same league. Just be careful not to kiss their asses too much,' he jokes. He's a tall French-looking man, with a big nose and a goatee. His first time at the stadium was in 1975 when he was five. He never saw the last season Red Star played in the first division. 'In life, a man can like one, two, three girls, but just one team,' Thierry says (what a philosopher!).

In the past 30 years, several clubs have claimed to become the 'second club in Paris', but none lasted long enough in Ligue 1. Racing, from the suburb of Colombes (12km from downtown Paris), had a notorious spell of six years in the 1980s backed by the Matra racing car money, signing stars like Enzo Francescoli and David Ginola (Racing used the 'PSG model' even before PSG did). The money eventually dried up and they currently play in the sixth division.

Paris has a very niche football rivalry between Red Star and Paris FC, since they constantly face each other in the lower leagues. 'Paris FC has no history like PSG; they play in front of 300 fans,' Thierry says. 'There is rivalry only because they have racist fans [ex-PSG] and we are anti-racists.' The Paris FC fan base surged when PSG banned their ultras from Parc des Princes due to their history of violence (and, well, racist chants). Several far-right groups joined Paris FC instead, a natural choice, since the two clubs merged before splitting in 1972.

Unlike their rich brother, however, Paris FC struggled with no money and no supporters: they had an average attendance of 900 fans in the 2016 second division, way lower than Red Star of 4,900. (To put things in perspective, PSG's average attendance is around 45,000 fans.)

It takes years or decades to establish a rivalry, and city derbies are non-existent in France. The national rivalry is between Marseille and PSG (*Le classique*), because of historical and cultural differences: upper-class Paris against the industrial working-class Marseille (when I was in St. Pauli, I watched *Le classique* on TV in a dive bar; Marseille and St. Pauli fan bases are connected due to their leftie political ties). The last Paris derby in French top-flight football happened in the 1989/90 season when Paris Saint-Germain took on Racing Paris.

What if they could create *an artificial culture*? If a Qatari businessman saw PSG as an opportunity for commercial advantage and geopolitical leverage, what would stop a Saudi multi-billionaire from buying a charming football club like Red Star, for instance? Well, probably the chance to make money. PSG's Parc des Princes is located at 16th arrondissement, a wealthy area close to the Eiffel Tower (*le seizième*, the sixteenth, is even slang to describe posh youth). Even Paris FC in downtown Paris (13th arrondissement) would probably be a safer bet for a foreign investor looking to make their football fetish a reality.

Saint-Ouen, on the contrary, is close to Périphérique, a ring road in Paris that serves almost like a physical separation between the glamorous city centre and the drab suburbs. It's a multi-ethnic district with no boutiques and zero Michelin-starred restaurants. 'We are a workers' club, with cheap tickets, and free admission for the unemployed, working closely with schools and NGOs,' Thierry says. 'We are a club that has values and heart, not money. To be bought by Qataris or Russians for us is selling our soul to the devil. We are a popular club and will remain so. If one day, we were doomed by this kind of situation, we would build our own team like Manchester United fans did.'

I played devil's advocate for PSG before only for the sake of argument. However, the truth is that Paris Saint-Germain is not an artificial project only now: they *have always been* an artificial project. Since their foundation, they were modern football even before modern football existed. Their globally famous jersey (the blue and red stripes taken from the Paris flag) was created by fashion designer Daniel Hechter, the club's president from 1974 to 1978 (the 'Hechter shirt' made its debut during a home game against Red Star in 1973).

Unlike François Hollande, who supported Red Star, Jacques Chirac, mayor of Paris from 1977 to 1995, and president of France from 1995 to 2007, was an outspoken PSG fan due to their representation of the 'Paris elite' (Nicolas Sarkozy and Emmanuel Macron are both PSG fans as well). And in 1991 the club was sold to cable TV channel Canal+, coincidentally the first big investor in the French league broadcasting rights (owners now for 30 years).

The Canal+ era gave PSG their first wave of titles, such as the UEFA Cup Winners' Cup in 1996, beating Rapid Wien in the final, backed by names such as Raí, Ginola, Djorkaeff and George Weah (who left for AC Milan). The average attendance of 16,000 fans in 1990 increased to 34,000 in 1995, but one blot remained the same: the stadium was passively quiet. I visited the Parc des Princes during a summer vacation in 2010 (one year before Qatar Sports came on board). They had just two league trophies to their name, coming off from a mid-table season. The stadium tour was basically made up of me, a dad and his toddler son and two other people (probably hipsters who would say 'I was into PSG before PSG became a thing'). It was a depressing visit, but not as depressing as when I visited Stade Bauer.

To fully understand all the Red Star motivation, it's essential to visit their stadium in Saint-Ouen, even if they were not playing there that season. The commute from the centre of Paris takes a little more than an hour to the Porte de Clignancourt Metro station. This is where Les Puces flea market is located, the largest of its kind in the world, a chaotic labyrinth of vintage clothing, antique objects and every imaginable knick-knack. If you're looking for obscure French football jerseys or a porcelain saucer, this is the right place. However, I had another destination in mind.

Instead of following the big crowd (of tourists and local people – the flea market is truly a Parisian event), I took the adjacent Avenue Michelet leading to the stadium, a strip full of stalls selling knock-off articles (especially streetwear, sneakers and sunglasses). There are remarkably few tourists wandering around this area and all the vendors are visibly of Arabic descent (they think, for some unknown reason, that every tourist is American even if you don't look like Alex Jones). Out of the *seizieme*, a croissant will cost €3 less than in the city centre, and a coffee is half-priced compared with what you get at the Champs Elysees.

Right across the stadium, L'Olympic de Saint-Ouen is a pub that Red Star fans have made their HQ since the 1970s. Like any respectable pub in the suburbs, it was fully open at 2pm. I tried to talk to the owner, a grey-haired man in his 60s, but unfortunately Red and Star were the only two English words that he knew. I tried my chances with the 20 words of French that I knew, but his mood was not the best (perhaps he was rude, or maybe just French). The bar is covered in Red Star posters, stickers and scarves from 'brother clubs', such as St. Pauli, Celtic and Livorno (in short, all the lefties). Red Star had moved away from Bauer for the last two years, since the stadium failed to meet the safety standards of the second division. The business at L'Olympic was probably suffering from the lack of games. Instead of having a drink and chatting with an old grumpy man, I took some pictures, thanked him and left. *C'est la vie, mon ami.*

Stade Bauer is across the street from the bar, and it has been the home of Red Star for over 110 years. The abandoned box office seemed like something out of a zombie apocalypse movie. Upon entering the reception, the room was completely devoid of human beings. There was a wall with information about the Red Star youth team's schedule and a glass case with Red Star trophies – like a mini museum. A lone scarf hung on the wall from when they took on St. Etienne for the French Cup round of 16 in 2015 (they lost 2-1). Nobody showed up to greet me, so I went to the dressing rooms where I saw benches and cubicle showers similar to those found at a local gym. I kept snooping around. Nobody stopped me.

After a while, I went outside and tried a door … it gave me access to inside the Stade Bauer. I was not even sure if I was trespassing at this point. The pitch had artificial turf, and the stadium can host 3,000 fans of its total capacity of 10,000 (an entire section is closed off by security measures, where it is completely full of moss, like a ghost town). There was a peculiar building behind the goal, shaped like a triangular school ruler (I understand my failure in describing it properly, so I strongly recommend that you look at the photo included at the end of this book).

Brazil played against Andorra at Stade Bauer, a bizarre friendly game in front of 4,250 fans a week before its 1998 World Cup opening. Brazil won 3-0, with goals scored by Giovanni, Cafu and Ronaldo. This is translated from an article written by Sergio D'Avila for the newspaper *Folha de São Paulo*:

> *The infrastructure was like watching Brazil play an amateur team from a village on a pitch similar to an agricultural fair venue (...) It had everything imaginable, from the official scoreboard painted with coloured pen on a piece of cardboard ('Brésil x Andorre', in a child's handwriting), to fans singing Segura o Tchan in a megaphone.*[25]

---

25 'Melô do Tchan' was a massive hit song from that summer.

The fans invaded the pitch after the game, as Thierry proudly tells me (he was there). Unfortunately, the World Cup Final that took place a few weeks later, France versus Brazil at Saint-Denis, was too expensive for him to attend. He is a Brazilian football enthusiast, to the point of considering Ronaldinho the most talented player he's ever seen in football history. 'He used to play for PSG,' I remembered. 'I respect the great players regardless of the teams [they've played for],' he replied, deadpan. I agreed to disagree with him: Ronaldinho happened to start his career playing for the biggest rival of my team (Grêmio – blarg!), and I would only respect him fully if he had not made such a poor choice. Seriously though.

Red Star don't have any big names attached to their history, with the exception of French coach Roger Lemerre (with the team for three years in the 1970s, before his tenure as assistant coach for the France World Cup champions in 1998, and as a head coach for the France Euro champions in 2000). Brazilian legend Garrincha was very close to signing with Red Star, way past his prime at 38 years old, and according to Thierry, 'he drank too much the day before and he was unable to sign the contract'. It is not exactly the story that Garrincha himself told during an interview for the Brazilian sports magazine *Placar*, as it follows, translated from Portuguese:

> *The players had to take in all their own gear for training, and the club only provided the uniform on matchdays. That was when a fat Frenchman came to me and explained that 'he was sorry, but couldn't hire me', as I was very expensive. I had already thought*

the club a bit slow and unprofessional, and after
that meeting, I just left. I didn't even say thank you.
(September 1971)

Even if it is currently falling apart, Stade Bauer is a historic stadium, one of the four football venues of the 1924 Summer Olympics. Red Star fans consider it a sacred temple. 'I used to go every day to the stadium, to see the training or the players because I lived in the neighbourhood,' Thierry says. 'I'm not a fan of collecting jerseys or press articles, but I consider Red Star as a part of me, and when I die, my ashes will be buried at Bauer.'

The stadium is currently owned by the Saint-Ouen Town Hall, and after Red Star president Patrice Haddad, a film-maker who took over the club in 2008, planned to move it from there, the fans vehemently opposed it (a full renovation is confirmed to take place in 2023). It was not the first time that a move from Bauer was proposed. In June 1998, Red Star was slated to be the tenant of Stade de France, provided they had enough funding to play in the first division. Instead, a few months later they were relegated to the third division.

When the team finally returned to the second division in 2015, the Stade Bauer was dilapidated to the point of not having a licence to host the games, due to its lack of safety and toilets (!), which are only accessible from outside the stadium (under the stands). Red Star had to play 75km (47 miles) away, north of Paris, in Beauvais, where my Ryanair flight landed from Lisbon. (Important travel tip: it is better to book a flight directly to Paris even if it's more expensive because otherwise you're spending one and a quarter hours and an extra €20 trying to get to your final destination.) Red Star's average attendance dropped and fans boycotted the games. I made the commute only once and I perfectly understand why they were so upset.

During my visit in the 2016/17 season for this book, Red Star were playing in the Stade Jean-Bouin, shared with the rugby team Stade Français. It's located just across the road from the Parc des Princes, a 15-minute walk from the Roland Garros tennis courts. Ultra-modern, centralised, and with tickets as cheap as €10, Red Star's strategy was to attract enough people to occupy its 20,000 capacity. The season ended with a disappointing average attendance of 4,950 (better than the 1,910 fans in Beauvais, but not even close to the rugby team's average).

(A big parenthesis here. Even if Paris lacks a football tradition, there are at least five historical venues to visit. Stade de France in Saint-Denis, where Zidane completely annihilated Brazil in the 1998 World Cup Final; PSG's Parc des Princes, originally opened as a velodrome, and renovated in 1972 (it's a phenomenal ground); Paris FC's Stade Charlety, opened in 1939 and easily accessible by Metro; and the Olympic Stadium in Colombes, home to the 1938 World Cup Final, and the stage for Pelé, Bobby Moore and Sylvester Stallone to defeat the Nazis in the film *Escape to Victory*. Who needs the Louvre and the Arc de Triomphe – am I right?)

Stade Jean-Bouin's annual rental cost is €1.3m, 15 per cent of Red Star's total budget for that season, which was 72 times smaller than PSG's, according to *Sportune*. The wages of all Red Star players for an entire season would cover Neymar's salary for a month only. Without money, a reduced crowd and no stadium, Red Star were struggling to stay in the second division. Again.

Red Star versus Amiens on a Monday night was not what I would consider a big threat, but everything changed after the November 2015 Paris attacks. At least a dozen heavily armed soldiers covered the perimeter around the stadium, in addition to a WAR TANK! Accessing the patio was only possible with a ticket (or convincing the 'friendly' French soldier that you needed to buy one). Every half hour of walking around the city, I crossed paths with a man holding a rifle. The Eiffel Tower looks like a war zone, and even the square nearby requires you to go through a metal detector now.

The €10 ticket granted me access to a section behind the goal, a total bargain considering that I paid more than that for a ham and cheese baguette for dinner. (Being a tourist without money in Paris is probably the greatest challenge ever.) The Stade Jean-Bouin is designed in a way that the fans feel like they are on the pitch. It must be an incredible atmosphere for the home team, with so much pressure for the opponents (provided it is not Red Star playing there, since their fan base is so small). The stadium was clearly too big for the crowd that was spread out from each other; I could hear the players loud and clear as well as an echo.

The noisiest section was near the ultras, composed of mostly young kids, holding banners saying *Resistance* and *Red Star, C'est Bauer*, and chanting for the entire game. It was a cold evening of 5°C, and the most insufferable football match that was ever played. I recorded a 30-second video with the worst sequence ever: a wrong, long pass by the Red Star defender, accompanied by a long kick from the

Amiens goalkeeper, followed by a midfield scramble, then a wrong pass by an Amiens player, a short right pass (!) by the Red Star defender to his team-mate, who tried a long throw that went straight to the corner. The ball was suffering.

'Every game at Red Star is for me a real pleasure,' Thierry says. 'But my dream would be a promotion to Ligue 1 before I die.' Red Star lost to Amiens 1-0, and seven other games, to finish the season relegated to the third division. At the same time, it's the only way Red Star are able to play at Stade Bauer, where their small fan base feels like they are giants. A stadium that one day I will return to, not during an abandoned day, but with the fans in the stands chanting and shouting. I thought about the old grumpy man from the bar L'Olympic de Saint-Ouen, smiling at fans while serving flat bottles of 1664 beer. By the Champs-Élyseés, I sat down and wept.

Next stop: Rotterdam, Netherlands
Distance: 447km (278 miles)
How to get there: Six and a half hours by bus
The best advice: Brussels is on the way and they allegedly produce very good beers
Soundtrack: 'Bonnie & Clyde' by Brigitte Bardot feat. Serge Gainsbourg

CHAPTER 12

THIS IS SPARTA

Sparta Rotterdam 3-1 Heracles
Stadion Het Kasteel
Saturday, 18 March 2017
Eredivisie (First Division)
Attendance: 9,712

Would you happen to know any Sparta fans here?
Sure, my boss! He normally attends every game.

There are times when Lady Luck knocks at your door. All my pre-arranged contacts fell through before my arrival in Rotterdam, so I took a chance by asking the lady at reception at my hostel. I briefly explained to her my book project, and not only was her boss going to the game later that night, but he happened to be a diehard Sparta fan. Marco Buitendijk, 46, a bearded, good-looking Dutch man, was in fact the hotel's owner, and a co-manager of the bar next door, De Witte Aap, once voted the 'Best Bar in the World' by *Lonely Planet*, in the epicentre of Rotterdam's nightlife.

Marco's father is Hans Buitendijk, a former right-back who played for Sparta Rotterdam in their last major title season in 1966, when he was only 19. Buitendijk had a promising career, having started six games for the Netherlands under-18s alongside a certain Johan Cruyff, as his son Marco proudly showed me a photo of both of them together. Buitendijk's footballer aspirations were cut short in November 1966 after his right leg was torn apart in a UEFA Cup Winners' Cup game against Servette in Geneva. He never played professional football again.

It was Saturday early afternoon when I checked in to the room; then I met Marco a little later and we headed off to the stadium for the night game. Marco shared a skybox with his friends, and as it happens, luck always comes at the expense of someone else's bad luck – it was one of the few times I bought my ticket in advance so I technically wasted €25. It is necessary to buy a ticket in advance due to the stadium's limited capacity of 11,000 that often sells out quickly.

Opened in 1916 as the first club-owned stadium in the Netherlands, the atmosphere was not exactly intimidating, even if the fans were almost on top of the players. It is as loud for a football fanatic as the Dave Matthews Band would be for a Slayer fan. Sparta dominated the game, scored quickly in the match, and the ambience was orderly and dignified. It was a good stadium experience overall, although it was not as frenzied or as cathartic as one would expect.

Het Kasteel (The Castle) is absolutely charming, a mustsee in Europe, and certainly an institution of Rotterdam architecture. Its name comes from the fact that the stadium has, well, a castle. It's a small building with two towers located in the centre. It used to be located behind a goal before a major renovation when the pitch was rotated 90 degrees, and the only remaining part of the old stadium is the castle itself, which is even more visible from the outside patio – from the outside, it might even be possible to walk by it without realising it is a football ground.

In the Netherlands, Sparta Rotterdam is regarded as the 'gentlemen's club', and it was founded in fact as a cricket club. Its origins can be traced back to upper-class Rotterdam society, opposed to the working-class club of Feyenoord, the giant club in town. In the past, Sparta always imposed strict regulations on membership while its city rivals were always a 'people's club'. 'The socio-economic differences are more a reflection of the early origins of both clubs,' Marco says. 'However, the main difference these days between us and Feyenoord is their ties to hooliganism, while our fan base have always been considered friendly.' Feyenoord hooligans have a notorious reputation for violence, which, according to Marco, is more evident when they travel overseas rather than when they are in Rotterdam.

Socio-economic attributes are not stagnant, especially in football. It might shift overnight with a rich buyer, and fan bases with working-class roots become increasingly 'gourmet' after, let's imagine, a Russian playboy taking over the club. For Sparta fans, for instance, what changed was their local area. Spangen was a predominantly white, middle-class district, which was overcrowded in the late 1970s. Over time it has shifted to be one of the poorest areas in the Netherlands, and 85 per cent of the population has an immigrant background, mostly from Suriname, Turkey and Morocco. Rotterdam is a very multi-ethnic city overall, and its mayor, Ahmed Aboutaleb, was born and raised in Morocco, leaving his home country at the age of 15.

The old white elite has mostly left Spangen for good and social mobility has led to only a minority of the Sparta Rotterdam fans still living there. The area became an abstract place and new residents seem to have no interest in the club (or football at all), even though Sparta increased their social projects to attract fans in the community. 'Our academy has several youngsters from Surinamese and Moroccan background, but it had little effect on our fan base,' Marco says. Sparta converted from being a neighbourhood club to become a suburban club.

Their supporters are either well-off in life or like to uphold traditional values, and this combination alienated the younger fans according to Dutch researcher Ramón Spaaij's *Understanding Football Hooliganism*. 'Local boys come to watch us [Sparta] six times and six times nothing happens. If you are young and want to riot, you go to Feyenoord, not to us. Sparta is too boring in that sense,' says an unidentified local Rotterdam supporter. Over time Sparta Rotterdam became a club with no success, no local community and no young fans.

The stadium skybox was like a parallel universe from the local area, with a spacious carpeted room, a glass window to prevent the cold weather outside from seeping in, comfortable chairs, free beer and *bitterballen* (aka the Dutch meatball). Marco's friend Jan-Gijs Klootwijk, a ship engineer and repairman, emphasises the family-friendly traditional spirit of Sparta: 'It used to be more a gentlemen's club, cigars and hats, and now it has become similar to the other clubs, but I like that it is still very decent and laid-back, and I can bring my young daughters,' he says.

Sparta Rotterdam took on Heracles Almelo, world-famous for once conceding seven goals (!) to Afonso Alves (the biggest Brazilian flop) in his side's 9-0 victory in October 2007. Upon the teams' arrival on the pitch, the PA system played Sparta's official anthem in Dutch, which can be translated to 'for better or worse, red-white is never lost, and years afterwards, we will speak SP-AR-TA', over an old-fashioned martial tune – the anthem is also used as their goal song, which I don't like, but it is not as bad as Feyenoord's odd decision of playing 'I Will Survive' every time they score a goal (ugh!). They celebrated three times, as Sparta easily won 3-1.

The club has all this pride of carrying its tradition, but having a gentlemen's background in modern football has nothing to do with having gentlemen's money. Sparta's budget of €11m is one-tenth that of Ajax, and seven times lower than neighbours Feyenoord's, making the club rely even more on their youth system. Their squad is one of the youngest in the league, and their academy is part of the top four in the nation. Dutch internationals Memphis Depay, Kevin Strootman, Marten de Roon and Georginio Wijnaldum all came from Sparta's farm system. Against Heracles, three players on the field were under 18 (Sherel Floranus was a frequent call-up for the Netherlands under-19s, but left for Heerenveen at the end of the season).

Dutch football currently always has the same script: a very young kid shows promise at a modest club; then he is sold to either Ajax, Feyenoord or PSV; then he is sold to a 'bigger league', especially the Premier League. I just came up with a name: 'Robin van Persie rule': he started at Excelsior at 14, then moved to Feyenoord at 16, and then to Arsenal at 21. There is zero chance that an upcoming star will stay long at Sparta Rotterdam.

Sparta are recognised for their football culture of passing and sophisticated skills (a Rotterdam version of Ajax more or less), the opposite of the Feyenoord style of *jagen voetbal* (aggressive tackles and pressure, that could be literally translated as 'chasing football'). In football, though, there is always room for fairy tales, like Thomas Verhaar who came off the bench. 'He was playing amateur football in Rotterdam two years ago and became our top scorer last year [in the second division],' Marco says. 'He was rejected by our academy when he was 14; but he never quit, a true fighter.' The awkward-ish tall winger debuted in the Eredivisie at the age of 28.

This was the first season of Sparta being back in the top flight, after spending six years in the Netherlands second tier – something that became uncomfortably more common. A founding member of the Dutch Eredivisie, the club was never relegated until the 2001/02 season, ending its long football legacy of 45 years straight in the league. That proved to be hard for the fans who were heartbroken, and especially Jan-Gijs. 'My father was 81 years old by that time and a supporter since he was six years old,' he says. 'A few months before the end of the season he got ill, and by the end of the season he said to me "if Sparta goes down, I am going too". He passed away on 12 June in the same year [of Sparta's relegation].'

Frank Rijkaard was the head coach of relegated Sparta, and when I asked Jan-Gijs about him, he snorted his disapproval. Nonetheless, Rijkaard's award for relegating a football club for the first time in their 114-year history was being hired by Barcelona just a few months later. (He eventually won the UEFA Champions League in 2006, before losing 1-0 to Internacional in the FIFA Club World Cup Final late in December. We won that for you, Sparta! Fuck off, Ronaldinho.)

Despite being a small club these days, Sparta have won six leagues and three Dutch Cups in the past (the best of the rest, behind Ajax, PSV and Feyenoord). However, without recent success, most fans come from a family legacy of parents who supported the team. It is a club with history, and their history is very well preserved. In a hallway at *Het Kasteel*, there was a giant picture of Jayne Mansfield kicking off a game in 1957 (the actress was in Rotterdam promoting a movie). A leading sex symbol of that era, Mansfield kissed Sparta legend Rinus Terlow on the mouth before kick-off, as Sparta lost 7-1 at home. 'The guy lost his cool!' I was told.

In fact, Sparta fans are almost obsessed with past and tradition. In 2016, they celebrated the centenary of *Het Kasteel*. After the game against Heracles, Marco and Jans proudly took me to see the artwork of two monkey statuettes seated on the balcony of the clubhouse, which according to the legend spread are there to 'guard' their players (also an explanation for Marco's hostel to be named King Kong, and his bar, De Witte Aap, the white monkey).

Then, I was taken to a members-only kind of a bar, a Sparta sanctuary of jerseys, scarves, posters and newspaper articles. I was immediately 'quizzed' to find Danny Blind in a picture (and I did!). Of course, I remembered him mostly from the fabulous Ajax superteam of the 1990s, but he played eight seasons for Sparta before. The other guy in the picture was Louis van Gaal (easy!), who made 282 appearances for the club.

Van Gaal was a semi-talented midfielder, and there is an entire chapter dedicated to his tenure at Sparta in his biography.[26] He was once speculated to be of the national team, and this is how van Gaal described the possibility of being called up: 'Well, I admit that I don't have a large capacity for running. But that is really not a problem, as long as there are players who are willing to run for me, as at Sparta. If that would happen at *Oranje* [the nickname for the Dutch national side] I would say: "Yes I'm ready for it." I possess the technique and the insight.' A contemporary of Johan Cruyff, van Gaal was never selected. (Later on in their careers, the two had a well-known dislike of each other off the field. Van Gaal went on to coach Ajax just like Cruyff did before him; and then to coach Barcelona, again just like Cruyff once did.)

As for Sparta Rotterdam fans, however, van Gaal was indeed their Cruyff. Even if he didn't win any titles while playing for the club, under his playmaker guidance they reached two UEFA Cups in the 1980s. 'I was only a kid at that time, although I remember that he was already a real captain in the midfield, always pointing out plays to everybody,' Jan-Gijs says. 'He stayed connected with Sparta through the rest of his career. I would love to see him as our coach.' The past is not trivial for Sparta fans; it is like they still lived there.

Another snapshot from this glorious past that I saw in the supporters' bar was a newspaper front page from 1970.

---

26   Meijer, M., *Louis van Gaal: The Biography* (London: Ebury Press, 2015)

The day Feyenoord's goalkeeper Eddy Treijtel shot down a seagull with a goal kick in a Rotterdam derby. Both teams, Sparta and Feyenoord, claimed to have housed the dead bird in their respective museums. It is fascinating nonsense, and the Natural History Museum confirmed the authenticity of Sparta's bird because the gull at the Feyenoord museum is of a species that only flies around in the spring. What a great investigative scoop!

The Rotterdam derby, at least nowadays, is a one-sided type of rivalry. There is a lot of history involved, but it is clearly more important for the Sparta fan base. 'The match at home versus Feyenoord is the biggest game of the season for us. We got promoted back to the top flight last year and winning the derby after not playing it for six years was very important,' writes Mitch by email, after he was not able to meet me in person. Sparta Rotterdam beat Feyenoord 1-0 at *Het Kasteel*, just a week before I arrived in town. Sparta were living in paradise.

When I asked Jan-Gijs about his favourite game at the stadium, he also corroborates the idea of the importance of the city derby. 'The semi-final against Feyenoord [for the Dutch Cup] in 1996 when Sparta scored in overtime,' he says. 'I was standing behind the goal, and I saw old men with tears in their eyes. We made it to the final which we lost to PSV at the Kuip, but it didn't matter, [because] we defeated our big brother from the south.'

There is a regional grievance between both clubs that has always been going on. Sparta supporters consider themselves the real club of Rotterdam. 'Sparta is the oldest, the first champion, they had the first stadium built, they first played internationally, the first club with sponsors on their jersey, etc., etc.,' Jan-Gijs says. 'Above all, we always played north of the river, while Feyenoord used to be not really a part of Rotterdam.' In the early days, many residents south of the river Meuse were farming migrants (before the docks were built), and up until this day, some of the Sparta fans still refer to Feyenoord fans as *boeren* (farmers).

The *club von Rotterdam* is an expression often seen at their stadium and in graffiti across the city, but it has been a long time since they were a big club. It would've made sense until the early 1960s, when Sparta won four titles between 1956 and 1966. However, since then Feyenoord overshadowed them in the late 1960s and started a streak of dominance in Dutch football, culminating with a European Cup trophy in 1970 (right before Ajax would hit back hard by conquering Europe in 1971, 72 and 73). Feyenoord is viewed as a 'sleeping giant', and their fans, the Legion, are seen as the most diehard in the country.

Furthermore, the city of Rotterdam breathes Feyenoord. The first thing upon arriving in the city by train at its modern Central Station is a Feyenoord megastore. When walking around the city centre, the club's presence is seen everywhere: bars, flags on buildings, sightseeing tours and flea markets. It is as easy to find a Feyenoord souvenir in Rotterdam as it is to find a city keychain souvenir. They really are *De club van het volk* (the club of the people), a fan base made of dock workers, blue-collar workers and non-Western immigrants.

Their De Kuip stadium (The Cup) is a few metres away from the river. It is a big monument with 51,000 seats, one of the major European stadiums. It hosted a record of ten finals of UEFA club competitions, including the 2001/02

UEFA Cup Final won by Feyenoord at home. I didn't have a chance to see a game there, but the architecture is a heavy contrast to *Het Kasteel*. Ultimately, Feyenoord represents the working-class people from a harbour town.

The largest port in Europe is in Rotterdam (where Jan-Gijs works repairing vessels). Because of its strategic position, the city was destroyed by the German aerial forces in World War II, when nearly 900 people were killed and 85,000 more were left homeless. Rotterdam today is a city rebuilt from scratch, an ode to open-air architecture, with many futuristic buildings (very different from the Dutch houses seen in the movies). Rotterdam is a fun and laid-back city, with a different vibe from Amsterdam, where tourism became centred around marijuana coffee shops and the red-light district, where half-naked girls display in windows waiting for customers.

The two cities are only 80km (50 miles) apart, but seem worlds apart, culturally that is. Rotterdammers are proud of being hard workers and feel like the capital residents are snobs and arrogant (they normally refer to them as '020', the Amsterdam telephone code). There are various quotes describing this discrepancy and the most poignant was written by Rotterdam poet Jules Deelder: 'Holland's money is earned in Rotterdam, divided in The Hague and flushed down the toilet in Amsterdam.' A Rotterdam legend, Deelder was a fanatic supporter of ... Sparta![27]

Some believe that the Nazi occupation during World War II had an influence on this cultural grudge. After the bombing of Rotterdam, the Dutch troops surrendered

---

27 He passed away in December 2019 at the age of 75.

on the very same day. Amsterdam was never affected as intensely as Rotterdam was. Even if Ajax is perceived as a Jewish club, journalist Simon Kuper is a firm critic of their silence and apathy during wartime, but also Sparta Rotterdam, which had the highest concentration of Jewish members in their city.[28] 'In the summer [of 1941] Sparta received a letter from the authorities ordering "Forbidden for Jews" signs to be hung over all food and drink stalls on its grounds. Jews are barred from sports clubs, but Sparta does not wait for that. They put up a "Forbidden for Jews" sign above the entire width of their main entrance.'

The animosity between Amsterdam and Rotterdam is reinforced in football. Ajax and Feyenoord hate each other. Like Celtic and Rangers' sectarian rivalry, the Dutch national rivalry is fuelled by cultural disparity. The *Klassieker* (Classic) goes way beyond football, encompassing the good with the bad and all the tribalism and violence that comes with it. Since 2009, away fans are forbidden during matches between the two clubs. Feyenoord fans once tried to sneak into *Het Kasteel* when Sparta were facing Ajax, and now they are forbidden there too.

As for the Sparta fan base, I wanted to understand whether their rivalry with Feyenoord is put aside when it comes to Ajax, considering all the bitterness towards the capital. At the time of my visit Feyenoord was leading the league, and fans were hoping to win the title after 18 years. However, in football, like almost everything in life, everyone has their priorities. 'I don't know any Sparta fan that would rather Feyenoord win the league over Ajax,'

---

28   Kuper, S., *Ajax, the Dutch, the War: The Strange Tale of Football During Europe's Darkest Hour* (London: Bold Type Books, 2012)

Mitch wrote me by email. 'Feyenoord is our rival, even if we haven't been really competitive for a while. I would rather them never win another match, let alone a title. I actually support Ajax as my second team.'

This feeling, on the contrary, is not as much reciprocated by Feyenoord fans. At Sparta, skybox, a friend of Marco's, was a Feyenoord supporter. He told me he comes from a mixed family and therefore went to matches of both clubs (especially as a kid). On a Sunday morning next day, we went to a bar to see Feyenoord beat SC Heerenveen 2-1 on TV. 'Most of us are not old enough to hold any grudge from when Sparta were our rivals,' he says. 'They are like a distant cousin for us. We don't care about them and we were even happy when they went back up [to the first division]. We have now three Rotterdam teams in Eredivisie,' he says.

Rotterdam is the only Dutch city with three professional teams. Excelsior is the smallest, from the north of the city (the three teams are geographically apart). They are seen as a poor, but warm, family club. Excelsior's best finish ever in the first division was ninth place, and their petite Stadion Woudestein holds just 4,500 fans, the smallest in the league. Sunday afternoon, I tried unsuccessfully to find a ticket to see them play Ajax (tickets were sold out for months, even before I planned this trip). There were no touts. No last-minute quitters desperate to earn a buck. Nobody was willing to help a foreign journalist.

Excelsior became a Feyenoord satellite club between 1996 and 2014 due to financial instability, the reason Sparta fans refer to them as the 'whores of Rotterdam'. Robin van Persie started at the Excelsior academy before moving south at the age of 16. According to Jan-Gijs, 'Sparta is expected to beat

Excelsior always, and they "hate" us because of it. Feyenoord is our big rival, although those games don't necessarily have to be won, since they are miles richer than us.'

Excelsior fans indeed consider Sparta to be their fiercest rival. 'The only big club in Rotterdam is Feyenoord, and I don't even remember the last time we lost to Sparta,' said an Excelsior supporter I spoke to, after declining to negotiate an extra ticket. He was dead right: Sparta had not beaten Excelsior for the last 12 games.[29] Including a famous game for the relegation play-offs in the 2009/10 season. Sparta scored in the 92nd minute, only for Excelsior to tie 1-1 in the 95th minute, as Sparta went a division down for the second time. (Excelsior also beat Sparta when they were first relegated back in 2002.) So yeah. They hate Excelsior now.

A day after the game we watched at the stadium, Marco Buitendijk loaned me a huge hardcover book celebrating the 125 years of Sparta Rotterdam. It was filled with hundreds of stories and pictures, including his father Hans recovering in a hospital bed from his career-ending injury back in 1966. (His father passed away due to lung cancer, exactly like his buddy Johan Cruyff did a couple of years later.) The book was written in Dutch, but never underestimate a fan wanting to convince you that his team is special. When you are born Sparta, you die Sparta.

As happens frequently to small clubs, by the end of that season Sparta witnessed their rivals Feyenoord end their 18 years of waiting for a title. A huge celebration in red and white took over the city, but not the one with the red and white stripes, the Sparta jersey inspired by Sunderland. Ironically

---

29 As of the end of the 2018/19 season.

enough, they finished a losing streak against Feyenoord precisely during the season their city rivals became the champions. It's not a trophy, but future generations will always be able to crack a joke at their expense. You can't always get what you want, as the song says.

After Sparta I was approaching my 30-day mark of travelling, but it wasn't over just yet. Rotterdam provided me with a great football experience (even if it wasn't the loudest), the nicest people to talk to, football lovers, free beer and delicious Dutch meatballs. After endless hours spent on buses, cheap overnight flights, and all the snoring a human being could bear at hostels, I really felt like I embodied a low-budget small football club. The entire project was always more Spartas, Rayos and Red Stars than Barcelonas or Bayerns. The trip became a celebration of small victories. Just like some graphic novel about 300 soldiers going into battle against an invading army of more than 300,000 soldiers led by an immortal giant.

Madness? *This is Sparta!*

Next stop: Turin, Italy (via Munich)
Distance: 613km (381 miles)
How to get there: Nine and a half hours by bus
The best advice: I read an inspirational quote once on Instagram: 'There is no such thing as bad travelling, only bad travellers.' Well, this is a complete lie, obviously
Soundtrack: 'I Will Survive' by Cake

CHAPTER 13

THE GLORY
AND TRAGEDY OF
IL GRANDE TORINO

Torino 2-2 Udinese
Stadio Olimpico
Sunday, 2 April 2017
Serie A (First Division)
Attendance: 17,882

Torino is arguably the biggest club covered in this book. They have more titles and the largest fan base compared with every other team presented thus far. Every fan I spoke with about this project could just dream of having Torino's glorious past. 'We would be in heaven if we had half of their trophies,' said Jim Marchant, the Hell's Angel-looking fan of Leyton Orient. And he is right. In Italy, for instance, only four clubs have more trophies than Torino, a traditional and much-loved club in the country's fourth-biggest city. Torino is also part of one of the fiercest football rivalries, not only of Italian football, but possibly in the world. We're talking about a club with an incredible local relevance. And besides all that, not even their most fanatical supporter would argue against the magnitude of their neighbours. Torino live in the shadow of Juventus.

Amongst all the teams in this project, they could not be absent in any way, even if I had to walk from Germany to Italy, which was almost the case. After the game at Sparta, there was a FIFA calendar break of ten days for the 2018 World Cup qualifiers, so I went to visit a friend who lives in a small town south of Leipzig – from Rotterdam via Cologne. From there, I travelled six hours to Munich by car to catch a bus to Turin (a good idea only in theory). The truth is, nine hours on a bus overnight was like 25 hours of 'Highway to Hell'. Especially when half of the passengers were families with babies screaming non-stop, and the other half were young Germans on spring break heading to Milan. The route included stops in the Swiss Alpine cities of Chur and Lugano, every time with a big fuss. I probably slept a total of 41 minutes.

When I arrived in Turin on a Sunday, at 7am, it was only five hours before kick-off. City bus tickets were only sold at news stands, so I was informed. It is like a ghost town on Sunday mornings in Italy, even in the larger cities. There were no cabs, no opened businesses and zero people on the streets. The only exceptions were, how wonderful, the news stands. Things don't work logically in Italy and this is the number one rule about the country.

Since I had to go to the news stand, I bought a *Tuttosport* as well, the largest sports newspaper in Turin. Juventus versus Napoli was on the cover, the big game of the weekend. There was also news about Chelsea's coach Antonio Conte (a former boss at Juventus), information on a cycling tour event and a story about AC Milan. And then, in a tiny obscure section of the first page, details about the Torino game against Udinese. One might read every possible gossip related to Juventus before finding a news story about *Toro* in the paper.

The *domenica a pranzo* match is a Serie A broadcast designed to appeal to the Asian market, inspired by the English Premier League. However, Sunday lunchtime is almost sacred in Italy (it's family time), so the allotted kick-off time faces huge criticism from several fan bases (but who cares about cultural values when you can sell more jerseys in China, right?). Instead of a traditional feast with family, fans have to opt for a pizza or *panino* from a kiosk vendor.

Luckily for me, the Stadio Olimpico was a ten-minute walk from the hotel. Unluckily, it was raining cats and dogs. At the box office queue, I was approached by an ultra-turned-tout trying to sell me tickets: the biggest cliché of Italian football. A short guy with dark eyes wearing a beret and carrying an umbrella. He looked like a comedy version of Joe Pesci in a bad Netflix movie. He 'offered' me tickets to the sold-out section *Curva Maratona* (Marathon Curve), traditionally infamous for hosting the Torino hardcore ultras behind the north goal. The entire transaction was a little dodgy: upon entering the stadium with a Torino membership card, I'd have had to go around a vendor stall inside and return the card to him through a fence.

I considered it too tricky, so he proposed a plan B, consisting of getting in later accompanied by the guy himself. In the spirit of dodginess, I told him I would come back to discuss this 'offering'. Touting is the main source of income for several ultra groups in Italy, and is controlled by the Mafia in some cases. According to an article in *The Guardian* in 2016, with as many as 300 matchday tickets, each sold for an average of €50 per game, each ultra gang could make close to €1m a year. Juventus president Andrea Agnelli was initially banned for one year in 2017 for directly authorising the operation (it has been ultimately lifted and converted into a fine).

Ticket touting is not a criminal offence under Italian law, but considered to be an administrative fraud punishable by fine. The ultra groups saw an opportunity of making good money for minimal risk. The culture of ultras at stadiums was born in Italy, by the way. Torino fans were directly responsible by establishing the *Fedelissima Granata* in the 1950s, a group that later on was followed by the *Ultras Granatas 69*, the first group to adopt the expression 'ultras'. They are famous and feared, with their giant skull-shaped logo easily seen at Stadio Olimpico. Granata is Torino's nickname, taken from the club's maroon colour.

The atmosphere surrounding the stadium struck me as being the most Italian possible, with a row of stalls with scarves, shirts and street food. I spent half an hour wandering and observing my dear fellow touter Francesco, and his prosperous business (I saw at least ten different people buy his tickets and then return the membership card to him). It is quite interesting that somehow Italy is a Brazilian microcosm, whether football-wise (with intimidating fan bases, and a lot of passion and drama on the pitch) or even culturally (with chaotic traffic, the bureaucratic routine and this frequent impulse to disobey laws). Anyway, even if I was tempted to watch a game at *Curva Maratona*, I respectfully declined being involved in touting.

I went back to the box office, out of the ticket tout's sight, presented a mandatory photo ID, and bought a €20 ticket for the *Curva Primavera* (Spring Curve), a section behind the goal on the other side of the stadium. The *Primavera* is the place for dissidents and the 'alternative' Torino ultras, such as the *Estranei* (Lefties) and *Statuto Mods* (well, Mods). And I guess tourists. *Granata* fans are as passionate and intense as one imagines them to be. They never stopped chanting and cursed at absolutely everybody: the referee, Udinese players and fans (who were right above us) and Torino players not performing well (which is the right thing to do except they had a very odd passion for Maxi López, who was on the bench).

Italian ultras' chants are mostly based on love and hate, as opposed to the 'English model' where chants are more spontaneous (and humorous). Seven out of ten Torino chants at the stadium were disparaging Juventus. Some fans would act as if they were 'chanting inspectors', looking for who is not chanting rather than watching the game. The atmosphere was not completely explosive, but a match played for peanuts on a rainy day didn't help. The carpet of synthetic grass separating the stands from the action also contributes to a flat ambience, even if my view of the pitch was rather good enough.

The unfortunate cliché of Italian football is that a lot of fans are racists; and regrettably, I heard the regular racist chanting directed at black Udinese players on the pitch. It's complex, and I cannot go into further details, but when

Mario Balotelli played for AC Milan in 2015, for instance, only to provide some context, seven different clubs were fined due to racist insults directed at him. Recently, AC Milan also played behind closed doors after their fans racially slurred Napoli defender Kalidou Koulibaly. Lazio and Hellas Verona have also collected punishments in the Italian league. I could go on and on. So what I heard was not just a mere coincidence, as clearly Italian football is not punishing blatant racism strongly enough.

The Olimpico was renovated for the 2006 Winter Olympics and its capacity reduced to 28,000 (enough for the Torino average attendance, not bigger than 20,000 fans). 'I have an emotional bond [with the stadium] because this is where I watched my first games in the 1980s, when it was still named Stadio Comunale,' says Gian Paolo Casana, ticket holder for 35 years. Torino fans have mixed feelings when it comes to their stadium. On one hand, they feel like they finally have their own home back, after more than five decades of sharing it with hated rivals Juventus (first at *Comunale*, and then at Stadio delle Alpi, built for the 1990 World Cup). On the other hand, the Stadio Olimpico is not exactly Torino's, rather it is a municipal stadium, owned by the city, just like the Olimpico in Rome (Roma and Lazio), the San Siro (AC Milan and Internazionale) and Napoli's San Paolo (in Italian football, only Juventus, Udinese, Sassuolo and more recently Atalanta have their club-owned stadiums).

The club has by consequence been prevented from renovating and they cannot make money from megastores, stadium tours or naming rights. Gian Paolo believes that the best alternative would be the purchase of the Olimpico.

'It is a modern stadium located in a convenient area for us, but the city should offer Torino a chance to buy it at a reasonable price, as they did before with the other team from Turin that I will not name,' he says. 'That would increase our revenue, as happens with other European teams that own their own stadiums.'

According to the Deloitte Money League 2017 report, even giant clubs' revenues, such as AC Milan and Inter, from matchdays (close to €26m each) do not compare to Arsenal's €133.6m, reflecting their lack of stadium ownership. For a smaller average attendance like Torino's, those numbers are dramatically reduced. The stadium has been renamed *Grande Torino*, and has the Torino maroon colours (*granata*), but it is not necessarily Torino's house. They only have a merchandising store across the road from the stadium.

The supporters are very aware of all this, although dislike the model adopted by their city rivals. They consider the Juventus Stadium artificial (especially after being renamed for sponsorship reasons) and made for tourists (especially for *Juventinos* from the south). Juventus fans disagree, obviously, as the old Stadio delle Alpi was very unpopular, and considered soulless. The new and modern arena is smaller, compact, with stands closer to the pitch, and more importantly, all revenue generated is exclusively for the club. Perhaps it is not coincidence that Juventus won seven leagues in a row after its opening in 2011 (on the same site of delle Alpi).

As many football fans may know, Juventus is the Italian oligarch football club, controlled by the Agnelli family, the Fiat owners that have managed the club since 1923. I met Gian Paolo in a bar right across from the stadium, a street named Giovanni Agnelli (the founder of Fiat, and the great-grandfather of Juventus's current chairman, Andrea Agnelli). Torino has always been more attached to the local community, having a loyal and firm *torinese* fan base.

Football fans have an overdramatic tendency to refer to their team as a religion, although Torino fans have a reason for it, and they have martyrs to pray for. 'We have a feeling that everything in our story would have been different if it wasn't for Superga [air disaster],' Gian Paolo says. 'Perhaps it wouldn't, since football is not like it used to be in the old days, but the tragedy is an important part of our history and keeps feeding our hope, I believe. It is easy to choose the other team in Turin, so we feel that supporting Torino is more like being chosen.'

Gian Paolo never says the Juventus name. When he does, he needs to drink water to wipe his mouth, a fun game between him, his friends and his son Nicola. He let it slip only once when I was there, clearly on purpose, as if that failure was better for my story. Gian Paolo is the main distributor for winter sports brands all across Italy. During a business meeting once, he told me, he vetoed a famous brand to set up shop in the mall inside the new Juventus Arena. 'Everyone at the table stared at me like I was about to break out in laughter, as if it was a joke,' he says. 'I wasn't, though, and there are other places to make money in Turin.'

I decided early on in this project not to 'interview' anybody, but rather have casual conversations during games. Associating Brazil with football comes up naturally amongst football fans, but especially in Italy, since the two nations faced each other in two World Cup Finals, plus the infamous (and tragic) day that Italy beat Brazil at the 1982 World Cup. That was the starting point for Gian Paolo loving football as he does, motivated by the *Azzurri* championship. The Brazilian squad had a tremendous impact in Italian *Calcio* nonetheless: Falcão won the league at AS Roma (1983); Zico became a legend at Udinese even if he only played two seasons (he finished second in the 1982/83 top-scoring table); Cerezo won the league at Sampdoria (and another four Coppa Italia titles); and Júnior, the left-back, was elected Serie A's player of the year in 1984, when Torino finished runners-up.

'He was one of the best players I've ever seen at Torino, a maestro on the pitch,' Gian Paolo says. 'I prefer players who are great at defending and attacking, and Júnior did both perfectly. He could dribble and score, but oh my God, he knew how to apply pressure on the defence.' Júnior is considered to be the most talented foreigner to have played for Torino. Brazil had an even stronger connection to Italy and Gian Paolo, as they played all their four matches in Turin in the 1990 World Cup. The fanatic Torino fan sold his ticket for Brazil versus Costa Rica in the group stage for the price of his entire month's earnings. 'I could have earned three times more when Brazil played Argentina [in the round of 16], but I decided not to sell it,' he says. 'Nobody in our city wanted to lose that game, and all of us were supporting Brazil because of our hatred for Maradona. I believe that only Napoli fans supported Argentina.' (Argentina won 1-0 as we know.) Torino and Juventus fans really hate each other, so Maradona may have achieved something spectacular: the only time in history they supported the same team.

The hostility between *Toro* and *Juve* fan bases is close to insane, and all around Turin there are walls sprayed with *Juve Merda* (Juve is shit) in maroon colours (there is graffiti trashing Torino too, although it is not as common). *Il tricolore non cancella l'odore* (The three colours don't remove the bad smell) is a very common slogan amongst Torino fans, a reference to the Italian *scudetto*, the crest worn by the clubs that win the national title. However, unlike the passive-aggressive relationship of big clubs with smaller rivals (that we saw in other chapters of this book), Juventus's hatred is reciprocal. Beating Torino is a high priority for their fans. Even if Torino haven't won a national trophy for more than 25 years.

The rivalry is ugly to the point of beyond reasonable. During a recent derby in 2014, Juventus fans displayed two offensive banners at the stadium that read *quando volo, penso al Toro* (When I fly, I think of Torino) and *Superga solo uno schianto* (Superga was only a crash), with the design of an aeroplane crashing, a reference to the Superga air disaster that killed the entire Torino team in 1949. Juventus were punished with a €25,000 fine, but a journalistic investigation broadcast by the TV channel Rai in late 2018 reported that Alessandro D'Angelo, the Juventus security manager, helped the ultras to secretly introduce the banners. The club denied all the accusations. It was not the first time, however. In the 1990s, while the Torino team was being announced, a number of Juventus fans would pretend to be planes, and then scream 'boom' after all players were called.[30]

---

30   Foot, J., *Calcio: A History of Italian Football* (London: Harper Perennial, 2016)

Just like religion is frequently used as a metaphor for passion, football fans have a morbid tendency to use death as a metaphor for their superiority over rivals. John Foot writes that once Torino's hardcore fans chanted *trentanove sottoterra, viva l'Inghilterra* (thirty-nine under the ground, long live England), referring to the Heysel disaster in 1985, when over 30 Juventus fans died after Liverpool fans pressed them against a collapsing wall. The rivalry is absolutely real when it comes to the Turin derby. On top of their ticket touting activity, Mafia and gang violence, when the Italian ultras are involved, it is because something has gone way too far.

According to *Granata* fans, they hate Juventus not because they are stronger, but dishonest. 'Serie A lacks credibility because of the institutional help that some of the other teams in Turin receive from the referees,' Gian Paolo says. 'The video assistant might help, but it would be essential to abolish the referees being picked by the league [technical director].' Gian Paolo refers to the 1984/85 season, when referees were to be drawn. Hellas Verona won the league and Torino finished second, which for him is not a mere coincidence (Juventus finished sixth).

Italian football has gone through numerous cases of match-fixing, in particular the *calciopoli* scandal in 2006, when two Juventus titles were stripped, and the club was relegated to Serie B. 'For this kind of thing, many Torino fans believe that winning the derby is our only possible title,' Gian Paolo says. 'It's amazing when we win against the other team [Juventus], but honestly I would rather win the *Calcio* [league] again than the derby. However, I know a lot of us that would not.' He probably has a better point than his friends: Torino spent 20 years without winning the *Derby Della Mole* (named after the *Mole Antonelliana*, a symbol of Turin), with the negative streak only ending in 2015. In the last 30 derbies Torino have won only once.

Another mantra carried by the *Granatas* is that Torino is the most popular team in the city of Turin. Juventus has the largest fan base in Italy made up of people from all regions, especially from the south (Calabria and Sicily) inherited by the thousands who migrated to work at Fiat. The majority of Juventus season-ticket holders travel from outside Turin, which led Torino fans to mock their rivals during a 2013 derby by raising a banner reading *Benvenuti a Torino* (Welcome to Turin). According to Torino fans, the reason Juventus built a smaller stadium is because there are not enough fans in the city to fill it up. Which is funny, but not exactly factual.

Gian Paolo, who is an incredibly diehard fanatic for *Toro*, argues that support is split 50-50 between Torino and Juventus, although Torino has a much larger fan base in the Piedmont region (where Turin is the capital). The main difference is that *Juventinos* are often newer residents to Turin (Italians and non-Italians), while the long-established *Torinese* population tends to be *Granata* fans. The club carries the name of the city after all, and its traditional bull crest is a replica of Turin's flag. It doesn't take a long walk in the city to see countless Torino flags in locals' windows or posters hanging in bars. It's definitely not bad for a club that won seven leagues many decades ago, compared to the 35 titles of their rivals. A pamphlet distributed at the stadium said: 'a *granata* is not convinced, he simply is'.

In the city, there are many sites connected to Torino, like their former ground Stadio Filadelfia, considered by many supporters as their real home. The club won five consecutive leagues in the 1940s playing there, and once went more than 100 games without losing. The stadium was being renovated, after complete degradation throughout the years. It reopened months after my visit in August 2017, with a capacity of 4,000, to serve as a training facility and to host games for the Torino youth team. When I was there, on the old mythical ground, only an abandoned terrace grandstand survived, cast away like a vivid memory. There was a spray-painted banner attached to it, corroded by decades. It said *Juve Merda*.

The Stadio Filadelfia is a 15-minute walk from the Olimpico (technically on the same street), a residential area with local bars, grocery stores and even buildings painted in *granata* colours. The Filadelfia was, ironically, Italy's first club-owned football stadium, and the nostalgia surrounding it is an obvious reflection of that unbeaten team known as the *Grande Torino*. A present reminder that many teams have history, but only Torino has legends.

The Basilica of Superga is a natural tourist attraction in Turin for religious reasons (this is Catholic Italy, after all). At the top of the hill, there is also a beautiful view of the Alps. It is located in the outskirts of the city, but a visit is fundamental to understand all the mysticism. On 4 May 1949, Torino's plane flying back in bad weather from Lisbon crashed into the basilica on the hill. The accident killed all 18 players and staff on board, 31 people in total, including the journalist Renato Casalbore, founder of *Tuttosport*, the paper I bought that Sunday morning.

Torino supplied the Italian national team with ten players in its starting 11.

When I was in Turin, it had been only a few months since the Chapecoense air disaster that killed 71 people, most of them from the Brazilian football club. Gian Paolo compared the two tragedies: 'This is something tragic that people cannot get over easily,' he says. 'But a few players from Chapecoense managed to survive, isn't that right? I saw it in the news and I believe it's a total miracle. The only miracle survivor of Superga is Torino itself.' At the basilica, there are Torino flags, flowers and pictures honouring the victims. The players' names are engraved on a stone under a huge cross. Catholic religion and *Granata* religion, all in the same place. 'We don't play against other teams, but against a curse,' Gian Paolo says.

There has always been an air of tragedy surrounding the club. In 1967, Torino's biggest star Luigi Meroni was hit by a car and died at the age of 24 (there is a plaque at the site of the accident); Torino went on to defeat Juventus 4-0 in the *Derby della Mole* the following week. The driver killing Meroni was the 19-year-old *granata* Attilio Romero, who would go on to become president of Torino from 2000 to 2005 (if someone needs an extra dose of esotericism to the whole story, the pilot of the Superga air disaster was called Pierluigi Meroni).

Ten years after Meroni's passing, *il capitano* Giorgio Ferrini, who was recently retired, died at 37 after suffering two aneurysms. He played 16 seasons for the club, and raided two Coppa Italia trophies for Torino (when he passed away, Ferrini was the assistant coach in charge during Torino's last Serie A title, in 1976).

We may want to sneak in here Gianluigi Lentini's tragic history, as he spent his entire youth at Torino before signing for AC Milan in 1992, for a world record (at the time) £13m. A few months after the transfer he crashed his Porsche at 200km/h (spending two days in a coma). Even if he never fully recovered his skills and talent, Lentini went back to play for Torino in 1997 and helped his childhood club earn promotion back to Serie A.

It has been seven decades of tragic events for the players and for the team. Something that has dramatically changed the course of history. Let's repeat it again:

1949 – Superga, the biggest air disaster in Italian history

1959 – Torino was relegated for the first time

1967 – Rising star Gigi Meroni died at 24 years old

1976 – Club legend Giorgio Ferrini died at 37 years old

1989 – Torino faced their second relegation

1993 – Gianluigi Lentini suffered a near fatal car accident

2005 – The club filed for bankruptcy due to debts accumulated

Torino fans feel like they have an eternal rain cloud over their heads, a sense of fatalism replicated on the pitch. After their last Serie A title in 1976, Torino finished second the following two seasons (behind Juventus in both). They finished second again in the 1984/85 season to Verona 'when the referees were not all in the Juventus pocket'. Torino also lost three Coppa Italia finals in a row (1980, '81 and 82), two of those after penalty kicks. In 1992, they reached the UEFA Cup Final, beating Real Madrid in the semis before losing to Ajax (on away goals!). Torino ultimately won the Coppa Italia in 1993, their last significant title.

All fan bases from this book without exception would die for a streak like this (cup finals, European final, league runners-up, etc.). Nevertheless, none of these clubs were remotely close to having a glorious team like the *Grande Torino* in the past (a true national pride). And all Torino fans are afraid of possibly not experiencing anything similar ever again. After the Bosman ruling in 1995, football can no longer be explained based on cursing. It is the money that rules the game, and Italian football was left behind compared with the investments from the English Premier League, Spain's La Liga and even Germany's Bundesliga.

It will probably never go back to what it was before, and Gian Paolo believes that the only way to keep the leagues competitive is to apply the same economic rules, even instituting a model of a salary cap for all the teams. 'If players knew beforehand that they could only earn a maximum salary no matter where they would play, they would rather choose a team based on their emotional connection with the fans, or with the city, even with a head coach they liked,' he says. 'Each team would have more or less a better chance to hire great players. I think the competitions would be more interesting as well, because any team could actually win.'

It sounds like a plan, but not in a million years is that ever going to happen in modern football. Modern football is designed for the big clubs to win every year. Torino itself was saved from insolvency by a millionaire, media mogul

Urbano Cairo, who owns TV channels and newspapers, like the *Gazzetta dello Sport* (the same that broke the *calciopoli* scandal incriminating Juventus on match-fixing). After Cairo took over, following a couple of seasons in Serie B, Torino returned to a European tournament after 20 years. They finally defeated Juventus after two decades in 2015. The businessman renovated Stadio Filadelfia, a fan favourite where *Il Grande Torino* made history. Above all, Torino fans started dreaming.

'Supporting Torino or any other smaller club is all about dreaming,' says Nicola Casana, 21, Gian Paolo's son, a very quiet fellow up until that point. 'I didn't like football when I was younger, but everything changed when I came to the stadium and saw all the Torino fans together; everyone is connected to a passion in common. It's good to have something to dream about and to feel hope, not only for our football team but for life in general. Perhaps it is a great feeling to win the league every year, but I don't know, it may become a little boring.'

It would be easy for Torino fans to see a glass half-empty, but they insist on seeing a glass half-full. It was then that Gian Paolo interrupted us. 'I'd like to try to win [the league] every year!' he says. 'When Torino wins the *scudetto* six or seven times, you need to come back here and ask us if we found that boring.' He is from a generation tired of only dreaming about titles. That being said it's not important to me if Torino ever wins a title again. I would definitely come back.

Next stop: São Paulo, Brazil
Distance: 7,840km (4,780 miles) from Madrid
How to get there: Nine hours by plane
The best advice: It was hard and I'm tired as hell, but I would do it all again
Soundtrack: 'The End' by The Doors

It hurts to set you free, but you'll never follow me.

POSTFACE

*It is the habit of suffering that gives
me so much joy*

In front of a crowd of 450 fans, VFC Plauen drew 1-1 at home at the Sternquell Arena against Brandenburg SC in the NOFV-Oberliga, the fifth tier of the German football league. The stadium reminded me of a municipal recreational facility, whose naming rights is from a local brewery produced in Plauen, a town 40km (25 miles) from the Czech Republic border (about two hours south from Leipzig in the former East Germany). In that same stadium, in 2012, VFC Plauen drew 2-2 against RB Leipzig, the same team financed by Red Bull that three years after was promoted to the Bundesliga and earned a spot in the UEFA Champions League.

The local team, meanwhile, went bankrupt and declared its insolvency in December 2014. Now they were back to the fifth tier, technically a former East German league. When I was in the city visiting my best friend, it was just a fun activity on a very sunny day, drinking Pilsner and eating sausages on the terraces. At the same time, when I thought about it some more, what happened with VFC Plauen and RB Leipzig only a couple of years apart from their meeting is a summary of supporting a small team: you either get rich or die trying.

We have always had the big clubs in football, the ones winning the biggest triumphs. However, the economic gap has never been so dramatic between them and the little ones. Feyenoord versus Celtic decided a European Cup Final roughly 50 years ago, and most likely they won't ever do that again. They are regional giants for the context of this book (Feyenoord in the Netherlands; Celtic in Scotland), but too small when it comes to Europe. In the very same week that I was writing this postface, Celtic were thrashed 5-0 at home by Paris Saint-Germain, while the next day Feyenoord lost 4-0 at home to Manchester City.

Being a traditional club and having a large fan base didn't stop them from being demolished by sheikh-owned clubs. If big clubs from smaller markets became irrelevant to the upscale new reality of football, the small clubs (from any market) are now invisible.

And I wrote this book because they are not, these clubs are not aliens: in fact, they are the majority. What I learned from all the conversations with the fans of these tiny clubs is that success is inherently relative. I have to quote Nick Hornby's *Fever Pitch* one more time: 'the natural state of the football fan is bitter disappointment, no matter what the score'. This is especially true for those of us supporting big clubs, though. Ironically enough, a couple of months before the trip, with tickets in hand, my team Internacional was relegated to the second division for the first time in their 110 years. It was degrading, and the worst day of my life.

However, for those supporting a small club there is no room to complain about a season of relegation, because they might be relegated again and again. No reason to complain about not winning a title because they never win a title in the first place. Yes, my team was relegated, but they also won the Copa Libertadores not long ago twice, in 2006 and in 2010. Supporting a big club was never a conscious choice for me, but inherited, so I think I was just lucky. At the same time, if we're being honest, at the end of the day Brazil is just a small market with no money to retain its best players, even if compared with Europe's little fishes (such as, let's say, Everton).

If football keeps doing what they're doing, then your team will be next. This huge economic gap that keeps getting bigger and bigger will not be good for the competitions in the future. There will be no competition without a certain level of dispute. When we take the unpredictable factor out of football, soon enough, we will just have clappers, and not football fans. We will have four teams playing against each other, every week, the entire year.

I understand that football is a business and this is part of its natural evolution (I'm not completely nostalgic about getting a bag full of piss thrown on my back from higher sections at stadiums, like they used to do in the 1990s). Unfortunately, though, the globalisation came at the expense of the pasteurisation of the fans. My visit to the Santiago Bernabéu, despite being a historical venue, lacked atmosphere and adrenaline and the same happened when I visited Arsenal's stadium once, and that is also the same with Barcelona's *Camp Nou*.

On the other hand, at Union Berlin's Stadion An der Alten Försterei every heart pulses with the stadium. At St. Pauli's Millerntor, we all feel alive. In the crappy terraces at Rayo's Vallecas, every fan is like a brother. Even the resentment at The Den shows that people really care. We're a click away from buying a Barça jersey in Thailand exclusively because of the people's love for football, not for fashion. I know it's a cliché, but football without fans is nothing.

If we think about it, globalisation has always been there, if we spend enough time talking to people (there is the Internet now!). The father of the Hell's Angel-lookalike Leyton Orient fan is a British-Italian who supports Torino; the Torino fanatic that will never say the name Juventus is married to a German whose family is linked to 1860 Munich; at the small Red Star supporters' bar on the outskirts of Paris, there was a scarf on the wall celebrating a brotherhood between St. Pauli and Celtic (the Antifa clubs); the Scotsman that I almost fought in a Hamburg hostel works for a Queen's Park ticket holder (that was definitely odd). Not even mentioning the shared stories of Andorra, *Escape to Victory*, Laurie Cunningham, Júnior, Pelé, by so many different people. There were coincidences enough to be passed as someone's fish story.

Football is the most popular sport on the planet because of the greats, but also of all the Adebayo Akinfenwas, Angelos Charisteases and Adriano Gabirus. It is not only about results, trophies and dribbles, but being part of something bigger. It is about travelling back home and keeping track of the scores of random leagues that I have no interest in, just to see if my new friends were happy. The majority of the small clubs in this book will have an unexpected win here and there, and many more losses, but their stories won't change much. Fifteen years from now,

Juventus or Bayern will have a dozen more titles, and these fans will be around supporting their own. Undaunted, following small tournaments as if they were the World Cup.

I asked a Belenenses fan what the reason was to support a team that will never win titles, after his team had just lost 4-0 to local rivals Benfica. He told me: 'Someone needs to do it.'

Yes, someone needs to do it.

AFTERWORD

November 2020

The world faced a global pandemic when I decided to translate this book into English. *In the Shadow of Giants* was originally published three years ago, in my native language Portuguese, and even if the stories covered here haven't significantly changed, it is interesting to see how all these teams are currently performing. Like I wrote earlier, I've been constantly checking scores and occasionally talking to the supporters interviewed in this book. This is what happened next.

Espanyol

When in 2017 I asked diehard Espanyol fan Carlos Iglesias what was his biggest dream supporting his club, he confessed that it would be winning the league against hated rivals FC Barcelona. Turns out things went quite differently from his expectation in the 2019/20 season. Not only did Espanyol face their first relegation since 1994, but the game that mathematically relegated them to the second division was a 1-0 loss to Barcelona at Camp Nou. It's definitely not easy being from the other team of Barcelona.

Rayo Vallecano

The season after I visited Vallecas, Rayo Vallecano got promoted to the first division, and in April 2019, they beat Real Madrid in La Liga for the first time in 22 years! Unfortunately, the team was relegated back to the second division at the end of the season. In regards to politics, in December 2019 a game against Albacete was suspended at half-time after Rayo ultras chanted that striker Roman Zozulya was a *puto Nazi* (a fucking Nazi), for his reported ties to the far-right movement in Ukraine. One might find the chanting a little extreme, but it is worth mentioning that La Liga had never suspended a game for racism or for homophobia until then. Rayo Vallecano won 1-0 when the game resumed in June 2020.

1860 Munich

Since the team's relegation to the fourth division in 2016/17, the Grünwalder Stadion is once again home to 1860 Munich. From having the worst occupancy rate of the league while playing at the Allianz Arena, they jumped to an average attendance of 14,953 fans (*Grünwalder* has a 15,000 capacity). The club spent the last two seasons in the third division, and the fan base had to witness local rivals Bayern Munich winning (once again) the UEFA Champions League.

Union Berlin

After many years knocking on the Bundesliga's door, Union Berlin were finally promoted to the top flight for the first time in the club's history. In November 2019, Union Berlin and Hertha Berlin faced each other exactly 30 years after the Berlin Wall fell. The club finished the 2019/20 season in a comfortable 11th place. Frank, Lutz and Juliane were reticent about Union Berlin becoming a club with a hipster fan base, but they are still attending the games.

St. Pauli

It has been ten consecutive years of St. Pauli playing in the second division; however, hated local rivals Hamburger SV have been relegated to the second tier for the first time since the Bundesliga was established in 1963. They faced each other for the first time since 2011, and in the 2019/20 season, St. Pauli won the two games (including the first St. Pauli home victory in the derby since 1960). Also, St. Pauli decided to part ways with kit manufacturer Under Armour and start selling their self-produced shirts, which will be released in May 2021. During pre-sales the club offered fans a chance to replace the club's sponsor in any wording they like. The most popular choice, according to the club, was: 'FCK NZS'.

Millwall

After being promoted to the EFL Championship, Millwall have spent the last three seasons in the second tier. They also reached the FA Cup quarter-final in 2018/19, but were eliminated on penalty kicks by Brighton & Hove Albion after conceding a goal in the 95th minute. Unfortunately, Millwall were also given a £10,000 fine over alleged racist chanting in their FA Cup tie against Everton in January 2019. In December 2020 Millwall fans booed as players took the knee in support of the Black Lives Matter movement. The club released a statement apologising and condemning the fans.

Queen's Park

Queen's Park were relegated in 2017/18 to the fourth division, but that is not what is really important about the club. In August 2019, Scotland's oldest club voted to go professional after 152 years as amateurs. The club started paying wages to the players, by offering their first-team squad part-time contracts. Hampden Stadium was sold for £5m, and Queen's Park started playing at the Lesser Hampden next door. The end of an era.

Fulham

After my visit to Craven Cottage, Fulham were promoted to the Premier League in the 2017/18 season, relegated back to the second tier (following 26 losses), and finally promoted again to the Premier League for the 2020/21 season. Wow, it is really a roller coaster being a Fulham supporter. What are the odds of being relegated again?

Leyton Orient

29 April 2017

Leyton Orient fans invaded the pitch to stage a sit-down protest against the club's former owner and the threat of extinction. It was the last game of the season and the club was relegated to non-league football in the English football pyramid.

27 April 2019

Leyton Orient fans invaded the pitch to celebrate the club's rebirth, as they were crowned champions of the fifth tier National League and promoted back to the Football League. It was the first trophy won by Leyton Orient since 1970.

Club Belenenses

After the dissolution between the club and its owners as a public limited company (SAD), the historical Lisbon club went back to the Portuguese sixth division (a district tournament). They easily won the league with 28 wins in 31 games and 146 goals scored. They won the fifth division next, and now they are set to play in a nationalised fourth division in 2020/21.

Red Star Paris

Following relegation, Red Star were immediately promoted back to the second division, and had to relocate to the city of Beauvais again. They were relegated again, making Red Star effectively a yo-yo club, with five promotions and relegations in the last seven seasons. In July 2020, their cross-town rivals Paris FC (the club that split from PSG in the 1970s) was bought in part by the Kingdom of Bahrain, which became a major shareholder. We may soon have a new nouveau riche in town, and it is not going to be Red Star.

Sparta Rotterdam

Sparta were relegated for the third time in their history in 2017/18, a season that included a humiliating 7-0 home defeat to local rivals Feyenoord. They got promoted back to Eredivisie in the following season.

Torino

Three seasons after my visit Torino came to a point of battling relegation, while Juventus won all the three *scudetto* trophies. They played nine derbies against each other, and Torino lost seven (and two draws). Torino's youth team returned to play at the reconstructed Filadelfia, and won the 2017/18 Coppa Italia Primavera (youth) playing in their beloved stadium.

ACKNOWLEDGEMENTS

First of all, this book is dedicated to my mother, Maria Rosaria, and my sister, Adriana, for their unconditional support, extended to me much beyond the writing of this book. It is dedicated in memoriam to my father, Bercílio Vignoli, who made me love football (and, of course, Inter) without ever telling me to do so. I love you all.

A special thanks to Maurício Renner for sharing ideas, his unofficial editing and the accommodation in Plauen, Germany (which I also extend to his wife, and my friend, Haidi Andréia).

I also cannot thank Emily Canto Nunes enough, who helped me organise the tour and for giving me the incentive to do it, even if it was an insane idea to begin with (I will never forget her support). To all my friends of many years: Leandro 'Bolota' de Souza, Vicente Renner and Hector Moraes.

For this English version, a special thanks to Alexandra Murphy for co-editing thoroughly my initial drafts, for exchanging her ideas and for giving me new insights where insights were much needed. She was fundamental to putting things in motion during very strange times in the world. Thank you, chouchou.

To Fernandão, for all the joy, happy endings and impossible dreams during sunny afternoons and cold evenings. In memoriam.

I could not have written this book without the amazing help of the essential people that I met during the different legs of my journey, at stadiums I've never been to and cities I've never imagined going to: Cristián González and Sergio Candel in Madrid; Luis Lessner in Munich, Frank, Lutz and Juliane in Berlin; Georg, Nick (in memoriam) and the Scarecrows Sankt Pauli in Hamburg; Alex Melnikov and Dan Crawford in London; Keith McAllister and everyone involved with Queen's Park in Glasgow; to all the members of *Fúria Azul* in Lisbon and the members of Gang Green in Paris; Marco Buitendijk and Jan-Gijs in Rotterdam; Gian Paolo Casana in Turin.

Last but not least, thank you to each of the 464 people who collaborated in the crowdfunding for the Brazilian edition of this book. A big thanks to Jane Camillin at Pitch Publishing to make the English version possible. I would like to share a beer with all of you. Cheers.

ABOUT THE AUTHOR

Leandro Vignoli is a journalist from Canoas, Brazil, who lives in Toronto, Canada. He worked as a music editor in his native country before moving into sports coverage, working in social media for the sports TV channel Sport TV. He worked as a reporter for multi-sports events such as the Pan-Am Games, the Olympic Games, and two World Cups as a columnist. *In the Shadow of Giants* is his first book.